PRAISE FOR SCOTT ODOM'S
STAND UP: HOW I LOST MY LEG NOT MY DREAM

"Being an amputee myself, I was naturally inspired by Scott's determination. After meeting Scott for the first time, I remember thinking his determination was not just in his words it was in all that he does. He has a much bigger purpose than even he is aware of. I'm honored to know him and am forever grateful that P.L.A.Y. could help push his dreams even farther."

—JENNIFER GRIFFIN, FOUNDER
P.L.A.Y. Foundation

"Physicians have the special privilege of getting to know innumerable patients during their careers. Relationships are often crafted during times of illness and great stress…the physician sees patients at their worst and, paradoxically, often at their very best…spiritually and emotionally. On special occasions, a patient will leave an indelible impact on a doctor. As his pediatric oncologist, Scott was just that type of patient for me over a decade ago when he was diagnosed with metastatic bone cancer. Scott's spirit, positive attitude and never-give-up approach to his illness led to his becoming an amazing cancer survivor who has accomplished much, both for himself and for all those around him. Scott's account of his unique cancer journey is a beacon of hope for all who yearn to know more about the young cancer patient's insatiable hunger for life and all it has to offer."

—JEFFREY C. MURRAY, MD
Medical Director of Neuro-Oncology
Cook Children's Health Care System

"Few young men have experienced as much adversity as Scott Odom. Hearing the word 'cancer' at the age of 14 is unimaginable to the vast majority of teenagers. Yes, Scott's story is one of adversity. But it's also a tale of hope and perseverance. I'm lucky enough to know Scott personally. I met him many years ago when we were both volunteers at Camp Sanguinity, a summer camp for kids battling cancer. Add this book to your reading list. You'll be inspired by his story."

–MARK "HAWKEYE" LOUIS
96.3 KSCS Radio

"A personal, yet timeless account of ambition putting the full court press on adversity. Scott's courage is contagious, and his success story is a monument to the power of the human spirit."

–PETER ROBERT CASEY
The Huffington Post

"If you've ever wondered how to turn life's seemingly crushing obstacles into fuel for your passion, read this book! Written in an easy, conversational tone, Scott's Odom's voice is clear and his message will resonate with anyone who has encountered adversity. Cancer patients and survivors, amputees, and the countless family and friends that share in their experience will especially appreciate this personal ccount of his journey. Scott's drive and determination are an inspiration and sure indicators that his goals will be realized."

–MEGHAN SEUS, MARKETING MANAGER
Freedom Innovations, LLC

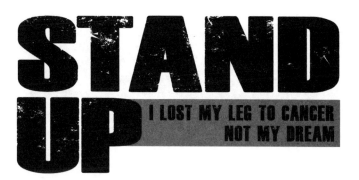

STAND UP

I LOST MY LEG TO CANCER NOT MY DREAM

Jackson,

Never let anyone or anything stop you. Keep working hard and know that with God, you can do anything.

God Bless

2 Corinthians 5:7

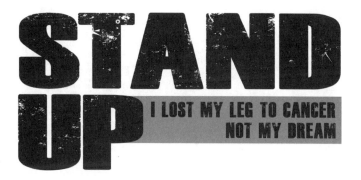

STAND UP

I LOST MY LEG TO CANCER
NOT MY DREAM

SCOTT ODOM

Brown Books Publishing Group
Dallas, Texas

Stand Up: How I Lost My Leg Not My Dream

Brown Books Publishing Group
16200 North Dallas Parkway, Suite 170
Dallas, Texas 75248
www.BrownBooks.com
(972) 381-0009

A New Era in Publishing™

ISBN 978-1-934812-95-2
Library of Congress Control Number 2010941781

Printing in the United States.
10 9 8 7 6 5 4 3 2 1

Cover Image by Nicole Hammons

For more information on Scott Odom and
Amp 1 Stand Up Basketball go to:

www.Amp1Basketball.com

I would like to dedicate my book to the

two people who were there with me side-by-side during

the toughest experience of my life: my mom and dad.

Without their love and support, I would not be the

person that I am today. I love both of you with all of my

heart and more than words can ever say.

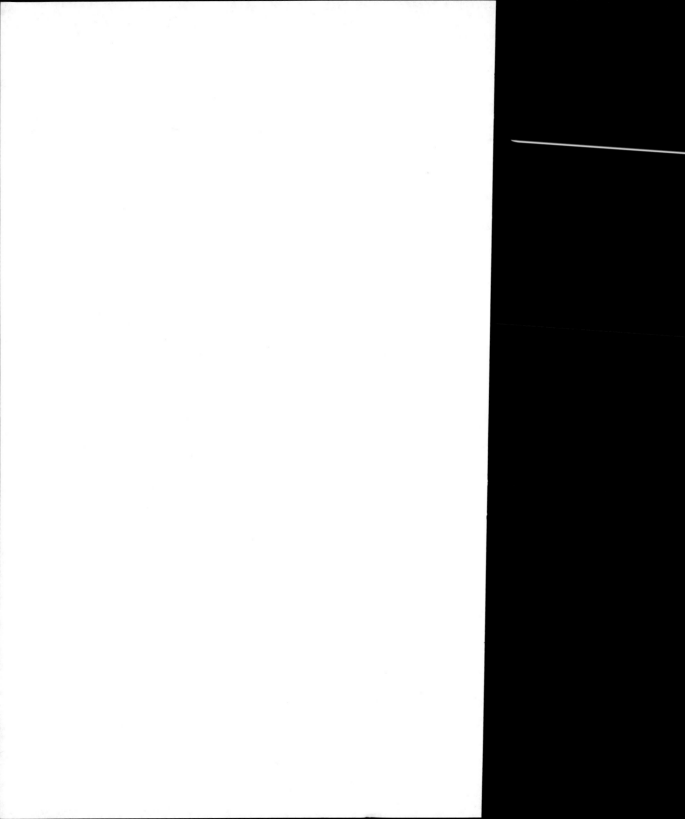

CONTENTS

ACKNOWLEDGMENTS

First and foremost, I want to thank God for everything. To some it may look like I have been dealt a band hand, but I am very blessed for everything that has happened to me. All I had to do was trust in Him and put everything in His hands.

I can't thank my parents enough for everything they did for me. They were put in the difficult situation of having their child go through a deadly disease—cancer—and they made sure I came out a survivor. I love them more than anything.

For my brother: for treating me the same when everyone else was throwing me pity, thank you.

To my family, cousins, aunts, and grandparents: thank you for all the love and support you have always shown me. Rest in peace, my Grandpa Hoyt and Uncle Tommy. I miss you guys and think of you when things are getting tough, secure in the knowledge that you're looking down on me, letting me know that I will be OK.

My nieces Summer and Madelyn: you girls are my heart.

For all the people at Cook Children's Medical Center, I can't thank each and every one of you enough for all the love and care I was shown. Thanks to Dr. Jeff Murray for treating me like a person, not a case number, and for believing in my dream. Thanks to all the nurses on the third floor for making me feel at home the best they could.

At his mother's request, I met with a young cancer patient at Cook Children's in his hospital room. Seeing the young boy lying in his hospital bed with a Texas Longhorn blanket, bald head, sports stuff everywhere, and IVs hooked up to him, I saw myself. After talking with them for about an hour, I was approached by the hospital psychologist, who told me that the mother I had just met with broke down crying because of how grateful she was that I had gone and visited her son. I was told that her son had changed his attitude for the better after meeting me because he saw someone who had the same type of cancer and was still living and chasing his dream. That same night, I bought a four-pack of energy drinks and stayed up until five in the morning and wrote the majority of this book. Kaleb Collins, that young boy, and his family are one of the biggest reasons I wrote this book.

A big thank you to Camp Sanguinity for having a camp where kids with cancer and blood disorders can get away and feel like a kid again. To the few close friends that I do have, thank you for understanding me and for letting me be who I am.

I want to thank Jeff Calaway and Andy Kane for being the first to help me with my book and believing that my story would give others hope and inspiration.

The best prosthesis in the world, Phyllis McNeil, who saw me for the person I was and wanted to become . . . I can't thank you enough. You always believed in me and told me I could do anything I wanted to do.

Thank you to Cynthia Stillar and Brown Books Publishing Group for being the first publishing company to actually hear me out and share my story. Just a month before meeting with Brown Books, I was given a rejection letter from another publisher. Brown Books has given me the opportunity to share my story with the world and I am so very grateful for their belief in my message.

My book would have not made it to print if it wasn't for Jennifer Griffin and the P.L.A.Y. Foundation. Jennifer is an amputee herself and her belief in my dream and her generosity to help me live out that dream has touched me deeply.

Thank you to all the people who have supported me.

Last but not least: Amp 1. Thank you, guys, for believing in my dream. For making the sacrifices with me when stand-up amputee basketball was just a dream I had. Tyler, Brian, Ray, Myles, Steven, RJ, and Jovan, you guys are my second family and we will live out what is now *our* dream.

A DULL ACHE

It started with a dull ache.

I was ten years old when I first noticed the pain in my right knee. I thought I was just playing on it too much, or that maybe I'd bumped it while playing sports.

Back then, it seemed like my mom took me to our family doctor on a routine basis. He would sometimes send me to other doctors. They all would tell me that for a kid my age I was very active and putting a lot of stress on my joints. According to them, it was normal to have some aches and pains. They said I may have pulled some ligaments in my knee and that the pain would go away . . . eventually. Another one I heard a lot was that I was experiencing growing pains and that the pain, to a certain extent, was to be expected. With the doctors telling me all of this, I thought I would be fine. Who wouldn't?

As I got older, I became more accustomed to the pain and learned to play through it. The pain in my knee became normal. But when I started playing junior high football, I noticed my knee pain got a whole lot worse. While running plays or running sprints, my knee would start to give out on me. Like the pain, I learned to ignored this too because I wanted to do my best, and I didn't want to be one of those kids who always complained if something was hurting them. So I sucked it up.

About midway through the season, my knee began to hurt even when I was sitting still in class. Deep down, I knew something was wrong. This was also around the time people started to notice that I was walking with a limp. But by then I was tired of going to the doctor. I was scared they were going to take me out of sports. I wasn't a star player or anything, but I felt like if I didn't stay with it I would never be as good as I was capable of being.

During football season and even basketball season of my first junior high year, I played through the pain. There were times when my knee throbbed and hurt so badly I wasn't sure if I was really hurting myself more by not saying anything about it. I figured that when my knee was really hurting it was because I'd overdone it that day or that week. After all, that's what the doctors had told me. When I was at a point where my knee was at its worst, I would go home and ice it. I'd pop some aspirin and try not to think about it. I wasn't taking very good care of myself, but I also loved to play sports and be a part of it all. I didn't want to lose that.

It was during our last week of practices, with one game left, that I finally felt like all my hard work and never missing a practice finally paid off. During the middle of practice one day, the coach asked me go to the other side of the field and run some plays with the A team. I figured they needed some extra people to run some drills, so I just went over and did my thing. The coach told me he was upset because none of his receivers were blocking the guy they were supposed to be blocking. He asked me if I was up for it and if I could knock the hell out of the linebacker. In my mind I wasn't sure if I could do it—this guy was huge compared to me—but I didn't want the coach to see that, so I told him I would do it.

I lined up and kept my eye on the linebacker I was supposed to block. The whole time I was looking at him, all his attention was on the quarterback. I looked down at the ball, waiting for the play to run. A few seconds passed and the play began. I ran in a full sprint over to him. I could see that his eyes were still on the quarterback and where the ball might be going. Just as he began to turn his head in my direction, I ran at him full speed. A loud smack echoed across the field and a chorus of sympathetic groans went up from the other players. I felt like I had run into a wall.

After the big collision, I came back to my senses and I saw that I was still standing and that the linebacker was flat on his back. I could hear the roaring of the rest of the team. The coach ran over to me and gave me a high five, telling me what a great job I'd done. That's what I love about sports: that feeling you have when you earn the respect of your teammates and your coaches when you feel like all your hard work has finally paid off. For the last game of that season, the coach put me on the A team, and I started as the wide receiver.

Basketball season was next. I was put on the A-team at the beginning of the season. It was a great honor, but I wasn't getting much playing time. This bothered me because I loved to play. About mid-season my coach moved me down to the B team, where I started and got a lot more playing time.

Spring was coming and that meant baseball season. I loved everything about baseball. I couldn't wait to get out of school and go to practice. I wanted practice to last forever; I never wanted to quit playing. This was probably the sport I shined at most, and my love for the game really showed. I was picked to be on the all-star team. It was the best feeling in the world to be an all-star.

Toward the end of that season, my parents told my brother and me that we were moving to a different town. I wasn't happy. I didn't want to move and have to make new friends. Plus I was doing really well in sports and the coaches all knew me. I felt like I had finally proved myself to them and showed them that I was a player. I was going to have to start a new school, find new friends, and start over in sports. I was miserable.

In the summer of 1996, my family moved to a three-bedroom, two-bath house on five acres of land in Joshua, Texas.

2

JOSHUA, TEXAS

August finally rolled around and my mom took my brother and me to our first day of school. School had already started by the time we got there. My mom wished us luck and went on her way. That entire first day of school I don't think I really spoke to anyone. That's how shy I could be—and still am at times. The only thing that really gets me out of my shell is sports.

After school, it was time for the first day of football practice. I was late getting there because I was the new kid and had to be issued my equipment. All of those shy, scared, and intimidated feelings faded away as soon as I stepped onto the field. A sports field felt like home to me no matter what town I was in at the time. I saw one of the coaches on the field and ran up to him to introduce myself.

With the season I had just come off of, I was ready to show these coaches and players what I could do. Most of the kids already knew each other and could tell that I was the new kid. A few of them came up to me and asked me my name and what school I came from. When I told them I came from Everman, they were all excited because they knew that it was a winning school; apparently Joshua was *not* a winning school.

About a month into school we had our first football game. I was the starting receiver on the B team, which I didn't mind so much because I was getting a lot of playing time. I was pumped and ready for the game. At the start of the game, we kicked off to the opposing team. When our kicker kicked the ball, I took off at full speed with my eye on the guy in front of me. He saw me and I saw him. We were running full speed at each other; it was like two cars playing chicken. I wasn't going to get out of the way and neither was he. Finally there was a loud *pop* as our helmets and gear collided. We both stood there in a daze, looking at each other. All I could hear was the roaring of the crowd.

I fed off of hearing that reaction. By the third quarter, the game was still tied at 0–0. The type of offense we were running was mostly running plays, but the coach decided it was time to mix it up a bit and throw in some pass plays. I used a few moves to break away from my defender. I got running toward the sidelines when our quarterback saw me and threw the ball in my direction. With two defenders around me, I jumped up as high as I could and pulled down the reception. Still in shock that I had caught the ball, I ran down the field. Once again I could hear the roar of the crowd. I had finally reached the end zone. I threw my arms up in the air with a feeling of complete satisfaction, still in shock; this was my first touchdown. I was on a kind of high that was hard to explain. I ended up playing a good game and we won 6–0. With a game like this to begin my time at the new school, I knew this was the beginning of big things for me at Joshua.

Throughout the season, I didn't have much knee pain. There were times when it bothered me more than other times, but I was finally starting to feel like things were going to be fine.

Basketball season came next, and I was placed on the A team. I had games where I would help with defense and then ones where I was draining three-pointers. The three-pointer was definitely my shot. About halfway through basketball season, the pain in my knee came back. While standing in line for a drill, the pain was so bad the only way to relieve it was to make it pop. I started squatting down over and over again trying to get it to pop. Along with the throbbing, there was also a new stinging sensation.

Since I was new in town, no one knew I had a history of knee pain. Since my knee wasn't bothering me, I wasn't about to say anything or give my history. The doctors had told me it was nothing major, and I wasn't about to be one of those kids who complained about this or that hurting. This was becoming so common that when my mom would see me limping she would have the pain medication ready.

With football and basketball behind me, the sport I shined at the most was just around the corner: baseball. With the confidence I had playing this sport and the attitude I had to improve myself each time I got out there, I had a feeling that this was going to be the best season *ever*. And, as it turned out, I was the starting second baseman for our team and one of the top batters throughout the season.

The best thing was that our coach's son, who was on the varsity team, would come to our practices with some of his teammates and help us out. I looked up to those guys. Playing varsity was one of the steps in my dream of becoming a professional athlete. I would look at those varsity jackets and dream of wearing one.

During that season, I hit my first home run. As I rounded the bases and returned to the dugout, I had a sense of pride in what kind of year I was having in sports. I had scored my first touchdown in football, I had drained three-pointers in basketball, and I was having the best baseball season ever and hitting home runs.

But my streak would come to an end when fate found me closing in on second base. My knee gave out and I stumbled. This was the first time in a long time where it hurt so bad I had myself taken out of the game. All the years I'd spent dealing with my knee pain, and it only seemed to get worse. I hated to be out of a game.

The next day, my mother took me early in the morning to go see our family doctor. We were told my regular doctor wasn't in, so we were going to see another one. He started by asking me the usual questions about what caused my knee pain and how long I had been dealing with the problems.

He pressed on my knee in different spots and asked me if any of those spots hurt. A few of the spots were a little bit tender but nothing too bad. After that he bent my leg and straightened it, asking me again if there was any pain.

According to this new doctor, I might have pulled some ligaments in my knee, or I might have been experiencing growing pains. He prescribed me some pain medication and then exited the exam room.

For the next two weeks I rested, plagued with the feeling that something was terribly wrong with my knee.

My freshman year during football, my knee pain started to show in my play on the field. I couldn't run full speed. My coaches, who didn't know about my knee pain, thought I wasn't giving it my all.

With tears in my eyes, caused not only by the pain but from the feeling that my coach didn't believe I was giving it my all, I told him about my knee.

I was sent to the trainer, who had a look at my knee. He did a few tests to see where the pain was localized. There really wasn't a specific thing or movement that made it worse. It was a constant, throbbing pain, and I had what looked like swelling below my knee cap. The trainer thought I needed to be looked at by a doctor and that I would probably have to have my knee drained to get the fluid out. He thought that was what was causing the swelling.

When I returned home, I told my mom about what had happened at practice and that I was told to go see a doctor as soon as I could. Neither one of us was comfortable going back to my family doctor, so we were on the hunt for a new one. My mom's friend gave us the name of a Dr. E. She said that he saw athletes and was well known in the area. My mom immediately called and set up and appointment.

3

THE DIAGNOSIS

A few days passed and it was time for my appointment. Finally I got called back and made my way to the exam room. Dr. E made his way into the room and introduced himself. Right off the bat, I felt like I was in the right place, and the big question mark on what was wrong with my knee was finally going to be answered. He had me lie down and moved my leg up and down, bending my knee and pressing on certain spots asking me to tell him when I felt pain. Given my history of knee pain and my symptoms, he wanted me to have an X-ray done.

After all these years of knee pain, it seemed incredible that this was the first time I was having an X-ray. I was back in his office within a week for the results. He told us he was concerned with a cloudy area he'd seen around my knee.

"Are you going to drain my knee?" I asked.

"It's a possibility, but I want you to have an MRI before we make any decisions," he explained.

I was devastated when the doctor went on to tell me not to practice or play. While he was still explaining his concerns with the cloudy area around my knee, the word "tumor" was thrown around. At that point, I had no idea what a tumor was or what it meant. He told me it was a possibility that I could have a tumor on my knee. It was hard to tell in his eyes how much of a possibility it was, but he requested that I have an MRI and go see a knee specialist by the name of Dr. G.

The appointment with Dr. G was a week later. The appointment made three doctor's appointments in less than a month, and I was becoming annoyed. But looking at my parents, I could see real fear on their faces. I didn't really ask any questions because I guess I had convinced myself that I was going to need surgery. Other than that, the doctor was just throwing around all this big-doctor talk that I didn't understand.

The MRI on my knee was an experience in and of itself. It wasn't like the X-ray where I just had to stay still and they took a picture of my knee. I had to stay really still for a long time. Not only that, they injected some dye stuff into me to make the pictures on the screens that showed my knee all nice and colorful. The MRI isn't a machine where you just lay on a bed all nice and relaxed out in the open. I had to lie down on this narrow contraption and stay completely still. I was slowly shuttled into the machine's narrow tunnel. For close to an hour, I lay in that machine.

This all coincided with my first day of high school in the fall of '97. I was nervous about starting high school because I was going to be a freshman and I didn't quite know what to expect. At the same time, I was excited because this was going to be the start of my high school sports career. It was a big deal for me. My main goal going in was that varsity jacket; I wanted one of my own.

On the way to school we dropped my little brother off at middle school. My brother was never nervous about anything. He was outgoing and had no problems making friends. Then it was my turn. My mom always told me on the first day of school to have fun and not to worry, I would be just fine. My mom, though, can read me like a book and can tell whenever something is up with me. Whenever I get really nervous, I get really quiet.

I walked into the school and headed to my first class. I remember hoping I wouldn't be the only freshman in my classes. When I got there, I saw some people that I knew as well as some guys from the football team. I felt better, and the nerves started to go away. I made it through two classes and everything was going well. I felt comfortable and was having fun. I'd finally made it to high school.

I remember it was some time after my second class and we had about a ten-minute break. I was hanging out and talking when I looked up to see my mom walking towards me. I was mortified. My first day of high school and my mom shows up? She walked up to me and quietly told me that I needed to leave with her. She told me that my MRI results were in and that the specialist wanted to see me right away. Not thinking it was a big deal, I followed her out of school and we made our way to the specialist's office.

On the way there, I could tell by the look on my mom's face that she was worried. I asked her if everything was OK and wondered what had they said about the results. "They wouldn't tell me. All they said was that they want to see you right away and that this couldn't wait until next week," she said softly. At this point, I was still convinced that I had managed to mess up my knee would need to have surgery.

Even now I can close my eyes and conjure up that waiting room. It was huge. There must have been at least twenty or so chairs. I also remember the greenery. It was all over the place. I remember thinking it looked different than any other waiting room I had seen, fancier somehow.

I signed in and had to fill out what seemed like a ton of paperwork. We assumed the wait would be short, considering there were only two other people in the waiting room, but it wasn't. We waited for close to an hour for the doctor to see us. I remember feeling tired and frustrated. I had been through this over and over and was sick of it: four years of knee pain and still no answers. I was convinced surgery was going to be my only option. Emotionally, I was drained.

As I worked my way through every sporting magazine in the room, my mom was quiet—a blank stare on her face. She told me we needed to be patient. Finally we were called back.

At this point, I was convinced the worst outcome would be that I needed surgery. That image of wearing my own varsity jacket was beginning to vaporize in my mind. I wasn't really nervous or scared. I was just sick of it all. I wanted answers. The specialist went through the usual questions about my knee. After about five minutes she asked my mom and me to come with her to the viewing room to go over my MRI results.

She walked us into a big conference room with a long table in the middle. On one of the walls was nothing but a bunch of screens to view X-rays or MRI results. My mom and I sat down in the middle of the table across from the screens. The doctor stepped out for a moment to get my results. While she was gone, my mom and I looked at each other for reassurance. Just by the way the doctor presented herself and the setting we were in, I felt like we were finally going to get some answers. The doctor returned and began placing my films on the screens. When she was done, there were about ten or so images on the screens.

Dr. G began describing what she saw on the MRI. She pointed out where my knee was and all the stuff around it. As she was explaining, she pointed to a black area on the screen and said that was the area that had concerned her. My mom then asked her why she had been concerned. At that point, she started to speak in what I liked to call "doctor talk," and I could feel pretty much everything going over my head. Then the doctor dropped a bomb. She said that with the findings on the MRI and my symptoms, she was pretty sure that I had osteosarcoma. When she said I might have osteosarcoma, my mom and I looked at each other in confusion. *What the heck is osteosarcoma?* The next two words out of the doctor's mouth were "bone cancer."

All I could do was sit there in shock and confusion. I had just been told that I could have cancer.

I remember my first thought was, *No way can this be true.* I was dreaming, and this was a nightmare. I was sure of it. No way could this be real. A month before, I had been at my family doctor's office, and he had told me I would be fine. The room was so quiet. My mother and I sat there, shell-shocked. Then we heard the specialist say that it may *not* be cancer, that the tumor could be benign. We were frozen. Finally I looked over at my mom and heard her ask the doctor if this meant that there was a chance that I did not have cancer. The doctor went on to tell us that there was a chance, but it was a small chance, and she was pretty sure it was cancer.

As soon as she said that, I had all these emotions running through me. I felt like that was it. I was going to die at the age of fourteen. My dreams and goals of playing sports were over. I was going to leave my mom, my dad, and my family. When I turned and looked at my mother, she had this look of intense fear on her face. She grabbed my hand. She was squeezing it as if I was going to leave her right that second and never come back. I could tell that she didn't want to ever let me go. I was sitting there, clinging to my mother, thinking that this was the countdown to my last days alive. My mom quickly asked how I could've gotten this disease. The specialist explained that it was just something that happened in adolescence. She said that based on my MRI, I had most likely had the tumor in my knee for the last two years.

Of all the emotions running through me at the time, anger was the feeling that eventually dominated all other emotions. I was angry—*very* angry. All these years I'd been going to the doctor and every time I was told that I would be fine. At that point, I wanted to charge out of the room and go to each and every doctor I had seen and give them a piece of my mind.

I guess the doctor could tell that my mom and I had taken this pretty hard. She told us she would be happy to step out and give us a moment together. My mom just held me in her arms—both of us were crying now. No words at first. What was there to say? Then my mom hugged me even tighter and told me that we would fight this *and* that we would win. She told me that nothing bad was going to happen to me. We sat there in each other's arms for what seemed like ages. Neither of us wanted to let go because we were scared of what was ahead for me.

How do you react when you're told that you might have cancer? How do you comfort the person closest to you? One thing her words did for me that day was help me to believe that, no matter what, I wouldn't be alone in the fight.

The doctor returned and gave us her plan for me. She said that I needed to have a biopsy done to make sure it was cancer. From there we would see what needed to be done. It was a very scary feeling. Ten minutes before I thought I was fine. Worst case scenario? *Surgery.* Then this . . . being told that the chances were very good that I had cancer. How do you respond to that?

So I sat there trying to think of the worst possible outcome. It's morbid, but it's true. Because when I heard the word "cancer," the word "death" automatically came to my mind. But there was also this very small part of me that had hope. Maybe this was one of those cancers that didn't have a high death rate. I had to know, so I turned to my mom and asked her to leave the room because I needed to ask the doctor a question. I wanted my mom to leave because I didn't want to make it worse, to make her even more upset. But I had to know. I had to ask the question. Once the doctor and I were alone in the room, I couldn't find the right words to ask her if I was going to die. Instead, I asked, "What's the worst thing that can happen to me?"

"We could lose the battle, and you could die."

To hear that from someone, especially from a doctor, hit me like a ton of bricks. I dropped my head and began to cry. I now had this feeling that I was going to die for sure. I couldn't stop crying. I was terrified, heartbroken, angry—all of the above. I wasn't sure if the next day would be my last, the next week, or if maybe I would die during this biopsy I was going to have. To get told that you could possibly die from something you have is a very scary thing. She had guessed that I'd had this cancer in my knee for almost two years. Who really knew how bad it was in my knee? Or where else it was in my body?

The feeling of having something in your body that you had no control over—and the belief that you had never done anything to deserve the disease—was a huge blow. The doctor came over toward me then and tried to calm me down. I was overwhelmed; tears were rolling down my face. I now had this feeling that my days were numbered. It felt like I could die at any moment. "I'll go get your mom so you guys can have a moment together and then I'll come back and let you know what we need to do from here," she said.

At that point I was left in the room by myself for a few minutes. I begin to feel this out-of-body experience. It was as if I wasn't there anymore. I don't know if it was because I was so emotional at the time or what, but my whole body felt numb. It seemed like everything around me was silent, and I was in my own world. I sat there staring at the desk with tears rolling down my face. Suddenly, I wasn't only scared of dying but I had this feeling that I would be leaving my family, too. Just the thought of never seeing them again tore me up inside. Then I heard the door being opened quietly. It was my mother. As I turned to look at her, I saw that her face was ghostly white. Her eyes were red and full of tears. As we made eye contact, we both began to whimper. My mother rushed to my side and grabbed me. Again, we found ourselves crying in each other's arms.

"I'm scared, Mom," I whispered hoarsely.

"I'm scared too, baby," she told me. It was best that we didn't say anything else at that moment because when we did, it just brought on more tears. "I love you, Scottie, and we will do whatever we have to to make sure you're OK," she told me.

Then the doctor returned and began to explain what needed to be done. She told us that she had already set up a biopsy that would determine if it was, in fact, osteosarcoma. The biopsy was scheduled for the next day at Cook Children's Medical Center. In the meantime, she wanted me to use crutches to make sure that I didn't fall and open up the tumor site.

While the doctor was off getting my crutches, my dad arrived. My mom had called him while I was talking with the doctor. This was the first time I had ever seen fear on my dad's face. He's laid back and rarely lets things get to him. He came right up to me and hugged me. He told me I was going to be OK. He was setting his hopes on the small chance the doctor gave us that it might not be osteosarcoma. He knew how upset and scared I was, and he was comforting me as best as he could.

As we left the office, it all seemed surreal. When I passed the employees at the doctor's office, I felt like they knew what was going to happen to me. I felt like I had this big sign over my head that said I had cancer and that I was going to die.

The ride home was surreal too. I remember noticing a landmark and thinking to myself that this would be the last time I would see it. When I saw someone pumping gas at the gas station, I thought I would never get to drive or own my own car because I wouldn't live to be that old. It was a very scary experience and something no one should have to go through, especially not a fourteen-year-old.

Before we got to our house, my mom stopped by the high school to tell the coaches. I stayed in the car and waited. About five minutes later, I saw one of my coaches heading to the car. He gave me a hug and patted me on the back. For a minute, he was at a loss for words and then he told me if there was anybody who could beat this, it would be me. I could tell he was choked up. After he talked to me, I saw him comforting my mom. I just dropped my head because it was a hard sight to see. I realized I wasn't the only one who was scared . . . we all were. I also believed that they thought that I was going to die soon.

When we finally arrived home, I still had the haunting fear of death hovering over me. A few hours later, almost all of my extended family showed up at the house. They came up to me one by one and tried to comfort me. They told me that they loved me. I still had no reaction. I just sat there and stared, a blank look on my face. I remember nodding my head a few times. All I could think about was the biopsy the next day. At the time, I truly felt that the next day would be my last on earth.

As I lay in bed that night, I prayed on the little hope that I might not have cancer and I prayed for God to keep me alive for a bit longer. I remember how wet my pillowcase was, like it had just came out of the washing machine. I finally cried myself to sleep.

The next day we made our way to Cook Children's Hospital. My family and I waited in one of the exam rooms for the surgery. While we waited, a very young, short guy came through the door. He introduced himself. "Hi Scott, my name is Dr. Murray, and I'll be taking over your care." I was a little shocked because he looked so young, and I was taller than him.

He began to explain what was going to happen once the results came back from my biopsy. He told me once I was in surgery and they did the biopsy, they would be able to determine right then if it looked like cancer or not. At the end of his talk, he asked me if I had any questions for him, given the circumstances.

"The cancer I might have . . . is it curable?" I asked.

"Yes, it is curable," he said. "And it can be beat." Hearing that gave me the tiniest bit of hope. I felt like that was what I needed to hear, that I could beat this cancer. My family had the same look of relief on their faces and they even smiled, as if to say, "We can beat this!"

Hours later, as I slowly woke up from surgery, I saw my mom standing over my bed, rubbing my forehead.

"What did they find? Is it cancer or not?" I croaked.

"It is cancer, baby. But Scottie, you can beat this," she told me with tears rolling down her face. After I heard those words I just lay there and stared at the ceiling. It was real. I had cancer. It was official. It kept running through my mind. I kept wondering, *How did this happen?*

In the span of one day I'd gone from a promising young athlete to a scared kid fighting for his life.

THE BATTLE BEGINS

The biopsy itself wasn't a big surgery, so all I had was a few sterile strips on my knee. I still had to walk around with the crutches though. By the time I got home from the hospital, my small town of Joshua had already heard the news, and we had a message on our answering machine from the Joshua paper. They wanted to do a story on me, given my circumstances. A few days later, a lady from the Joshua paper came to my house to interview my mom and me. I had mixed emotions about the interview because on one hand it was neat that I was going to be in the paper, but on the other I was going to be in the paper because I had cancer. In the end, the interview wasn't about how I felt about the cancer, but about all that I had accomplished and my dreams for the future.

That was when it hit me: I still wanted to be a professional athlete. Even though I was facing a life-threatening disease, my love for sports was alive and well. It was the one and only thing I ever saw myself doing. Facing what I was facing—at the tender age of fourteen—I still wanted to play no matter what the cost. I took that same passion and drive for sports and focused it on the road ahead of me. I'm not going to say I wasn't still scared to death, but I had the feeling that I would do whatever I had to do to beat the cancer and get back to what I loved most—sports.

The following day we made our way back up to Cook Children's. The next step for me was another surgery. The surgery was to put in a double port (a tube in my chest) connected to my veins to receive chemotherapy. Instead of sticking a needle in my veins each time, there would be the port. Without it, the chemo would have eventually ruptured my veins. Barely a couple of weeks had passed and I was already going to have to have another surgery. It seemed like everything was moving so fast, and I had no control over what was happening to me. It was a terrible feeling.

All I knew was that I was going to do whatever Dr. Murray wanted me to do. From the start I put my faith and trust in his hands. I wasn't sure if I was going to make it from one week to the next, but I wanted to do everything possible to beat the disease. I remember waking up from the double port surgery and finally feeling pain. The upper right side of my chest was now all bandaged. When the day finally came to take the dressing off, I was shocked by what I saw. Something foreign was lodged in my body, sticking out a good inch or so. I felt that familiar feeling of losing control of my life, along with the thought that those might be my final days.

My parents and friends kept asking me if I was alright and if there was anything that they could do. All I wanted was the cancer out of my body, but I knew nobody could do that for me. At the time, it seemed like there was nothing that could make everything all better. I would just tell my mom over and over again that I was scared. And now, looking back at it, I realize how hard it must have been for my mother. How do you respond when your own child, who is facing a life-threatening disease, tells you he's scared? But I also remember that no matter what she said, I always felt a slight bit of comfort knowing that she and the rest of my family were there by my side and that they were fighting alongside me.

Days passed after my port placement, and I was scheduled to start my first round of chemotherapy. I tried to prepare myself for it. On television you always saw someone on chemotherapy looking all weak and sick as if they had no life left in them. I was wondering if I was going to experience any pain. How long I would be on it? How sick was I going to get? Would I even make it through the first round? How much pain would I experience? I had so many questions running through my head; I felt like I had this big question mark on my life. When I would imagine what my life would be like when I got older, I never pictured me going through cancer and fearing for my life day after day.

It was now August 1997 and we arrived at the hospital. This time, we had to go through registration to admit me into the hospital. The reason I had to be admitted was because the chemotherapy I was taking was some hardcore stuff, and that type of chemo took place over a five-day session. Even though I had child-life specialist talk to me and tell me what chemotherapy was all about, I still had a ton of questions. Chief among them was: is this stuff going to kill me?

The room I'd be in for the next five days was small with a hospital bed, a television in the upper corner, a food tray, and a small recliner for guests. The nurse came in with a big smile and introduced herself and told me that she would be taking care of me while I was here. Just the way she came off as a caring, fun, and normal person made me feel a little bit better. After the usual checkup stuff, which I was now becoming accustomed to, she put some cream on my port. She told me the cream would numb my skin so that when they stuck me with the needle that was connected to the IV to allow the chemotherapy to run through, I wouldn't feel it. It was to be on my skin for at least a half an hour before she could apply the line and begin the chemo drip.

My mom was there with me, and I could tell she was just as nervous, if not more so, than me. I tried to play it cool and act like I was doing well just so she would feel better. The nurse came in and brought this big glass bottle filled with clear liquid. It looked like decorative glass with some water in it.

"Here is your chemo, Scott," the nurse said. It looked like I was getting the top-of-the-line chemotherapy.

"So it's just going to run through me like an IV?" I asked.

"Yes, you won't feel any pain, I promise," she chuckled. I asked her if I would throw up. "Don't worry, some kids get sicker than others and some don't get sick at all. We will just have to wait and see how it affects you," she explained.

This is it, I thought to myself as I stared up at the big glass bottle. An hour or so went by, and I was still feeling the same. I wasn't feeling sick, and I wasn't feeling any different. After chemo, a group of my friends from Joshua came up to the hospital to visit with me. I still felt like things were pretty normal. I remember all of us joking and goofing off. We walked around the hospital and checked out the playroom. I even ate a big lunch with them and was feeling fine. "Man, this chemotherapy stuff isn't bad at all. This is going to be easy," I remember telling one of my friends. They didn't stay very long, but my dad arrived from work a bit later. We were all in my room watching whatever was on the television at the time. This was going to get boring real fast, I could tell, but at least I wasn't getting sick or feeling bad.

It was at this point, while lying in the bed, that I started to feel a little strange. Kind of nauseated and sick to my stomach. I didn't think much about it; I just figured I'd eaten too much with my friends. Then, out of nowhere, it hit me. I quickly got up and ran to the toilet. I began to vomit. After I was done, I came out to see my parents staring at me.

"Are you OK, Scott?" my mom asked.

"I feel better now," I said. "I think I ate too much earlier. I just need to lie down."

Not even ten minutes went by and I was back in the bathroom. I vomited a good five or six times in a very short time frame. At about the fourth time, my emotions got the best of me, and I began to hyper-ventilate. I was crying heavily and felt scared all over again. I didn't know what was going on or if I could handle the chemo or not. My parents watched me go through this, extremely scared and worried about me. The nurse was in there with me too, caring for me as best she could. I could hear my dad comforting my mom as she started to cry.

Finally, hours later, I lay in the bed feeling like I had just run a marathon. I was out of energy and felt weak all over. My face was dry from the salt in the tears I had cried. I lay there motionless, not knowing what to do. My mom sat in the recliner beside my bed and held my hand. For the next five days that's all it was—chemo and then getting sick. I had never been so sick in my life, throwing up a minimum of three times a day. Not eating or drinking. Nothing sounded good and, if I did try to eat a little, it just came right back up. I remember on my fifth day my body felt like it had been to hell and back.

I came out of that hospital a different person. I wasn't the same Scott who was active and ready for anything. I was extremely weak and looked as if the life had been taken right out of me. I was told to rest at home for a few days and then I was to go right back to the hospital and begin another round of chemotherapy. This meant that just as I recovered from the last session I had to get knocked right back down again. The reason for this back and forth was that they wanted to attack the tumor in my leg hard and fast before the cancer could spread. The tumor I had usually spreads—and when it spreads, it goes to the lungs. This was a very scary thought on top of what I was already going through. But, luckily for me, none of the tests came back positive for signs of cancer in my lungs.

That didn't necessarily mean that there might not be just the tiniest speck in my lungs. So, to be on the safe side, I went through the hardcore chemo. I was scheduled to go through this routine for about two months and then I was told I would have some type of surgery to get the tumor out of my leg. Weeks into the therapy, it didn't get any easier. Some of my sessions were only three days long; others were five, like the first time. I was taking many different types of chemotherapies.

I began to notice how the chemo was affecting my body. Not just the obvious side effects like being sick all the time, but other things were affected too. One effect was on my sense of smell. The scent of the hospital bedding would automatically set me off, as would anyone entering the room wearing strong cologne or perfume.

Soon, knowing that I was going to be there for days at a time, I started to bring my own linen. I even brought some video games to play and hooked them up to the television to give me some kind of entertainment. The more I came to the hospital, the more stuff from home I would bring with me to make it more comfortable. My sense of smell got so strong that I would be sound asleep in the bed and wake up when the cafeteria guy arrived at my door with the food tray. I would get this sick feeling in my stomach. I told my mom to tell them not to even bring in the food tray at all. I never ate the hospital food. No food sounded good at that time, especially not hospital food, and just thinking about it would set me off.

Because I stayed sick for most of the time, this meant I couldn't really be around too many people. The chemotherapy was not only trying to kill the tumor but was also killing all the other cells in my body. From white blood cells to platelets, it was going after everything. Usually after each five-day chemo session, I had to take a shot in my leg for up to two weeks to help build up my white blood count. As for platelets, these are the guys that help prevent bleeding. So when you get a paper cut, your platelets come to the aid and stop the bleeding, forming a scab and all that good stuff. Well, since I was having everything in my body killed, I had to be very careful. If I was to get a cut, it could be hard to stop the bleeding. Even though nothing like that ever happened, my platelet count would sometimes be so low that I would need a blood transfusion. My body was going through a lot. It wasn't only a kind of physical breakdown that I was going through, but an emotional one too.

A good day for me would be not getting sick. If I ate just a small piece of anything, that was icing on the cake. But there were very few of those days. Being a sports guy, I was definitely what you would call superstitious. I had my routine of things I would do to help me feel like I was beating this disease. The main one would be the way I would lie or sit in the bed. Being that my tumor was right below my knee, it came to my crazy head that when I lay in bed I had to always keep my knees bent. I became convinced that if my knees were bent, the tumor couldn't spread up to any other part of my body. If I was lying in bed with my legs straight, on the other hand, the tumor had a straight shot of going wherever it wanted. Call me crazy, but I didn't want to take any chances.

Another superstition I had was with the way I let my hands rest. I always had to have my thumb in contact with either my index finger or my palm, either making a first or not. I did this because when my thumb was not in contact with anything and my other fingers were slightly bent, it would make something resembling the letter C. And at that time, the letter C meant *cancer* to me. I didn't want to have anything resemble that letter or remind me of cancer. I was trying anything and everything I could think of to beat this thing.

For the first month or two, I lived at the hospital. When I wasn't receiving chemo, I was at the hematology and oncology clinics getting my counts checked, which meant having my blood drawn once a week or more often. At times, I would have to stay at the clinic for the entire day either to get a blood transfusion because my blood count was so low, or to run test such as X-rays, MRIs, or other tests. Such is the life of a cancer patient.

5

THINGS CHANGE

It was hitting me how much my life had changed. I had gone from a kid who could play from sunup to sundown to a kid fighting for his life. My weight had dropped dramatically. I was hardly eating. I went from 140 pounds to less than 120—and I had been skinny to begin with. I still had my hair, though, and I was hoping I might be one of the lucky ones they talk about who don't lose their hair.

They told me some kids lose their hair and some don't. I guess that's why the true reality of being a cancer patient never hit me until I lost my hair. I mean, I knew I had cancer; I was sicker than a dog. But when you picture someone with cancer, you picture them with a bald head. It was when I was at the hospital receiving one of my chemotherapy treatments that I first noticed that my hair was falling out.

I remember I was lying in bed watching whatever was on TV at the time. I hardly ever moved and, if I did, it was to either go to the bathroom or to just sit up for a little while. My dad usually arrived at the hospital right after he got off work. Sometimes my brother was with him, and other times he would just stay at the house by himself. When my dad came up to the hospital, this time he had brought food with him. Whenever I got a craving it was blessing because most of the time, nothing sounded good. I seem to remember the craving that time was for a turkey and ham sub.

He brought the food to me, and when I finally sat up my mom leaned over to fix my hair. I turned to see this look on her face that was positively indescribable. "Your hair's falling out," she whispered. I turned back to look at my pillow; there was hair everywhere. I ran my hand through my hair and more came out. I was speechless, frozen. It was one of those moments I will never forget. It seemed as though I was having them every day. "Do you want to shave your head?" asked my mom. I told her no, that I wanted to wait. But wait for what? Honestly, I wasn't sure. Maybe I wanted to keep the hair I had left for as long as I could. Who knows? That was the point where I began to see myself as a different person.

I mean, I knew I was sick and that I had cancer, but now when I looked in a mirror, I saw this sick "cancer kid." My self-esteem took a real nosedive at that point. I started wearing hats everywhere I went because I was embarrassed. It was probably a couple of days after we left the hospital when I told my mom to just go ahead and shave it all off. Later, while my mom was shaving my head, I remember watching it fall to the ground, clump by clump. I had the sense that my hair was never going to come back. The whole time my mom was saying how beautiful my head was and how cute I looked bald. Of course, part of me knew she was just saying that because she was my mom but still, it is nice to hear those words when you're at your lowest of lows.

Now, as a bald kid, whenever I looked in the mirror I saw Death. I was skin and bones, pale as a ghost, and had no hair. My reflection looked nothing like me, and to me it was like death was taking over my body. I hated to see myself in mirrors, and I was very self-conscious about the way I looked. The only time I felt somewhat normal was when I wore a hat.

Soon I discovered that the hair on my head was not the only hair I would be losing. My hair fell out everywhere: my eyebrows, eyelashes, the hair on my legs and, well, you know . . . Suddenly, my body was a no-hair zone.

The chemotherapy lifestyle lasted about two months. I was hardly around anybody except for the few visitors that came to see me in the hospital. But being so sick, I wasn't the best of company. In fact, most of the time, I didn't even want any company. As the days passed, I began to feel like people were forgetting about me or that they were disgusted by my looks and avoided seeing me.

I was told that I was to have another MRI to see if the chemotherapy was working. I would also have a bone scan, an X-ray, and other tests. I kept thinking to myself, *This stuff better be working. It is making me sicker than a dog. If it's not working, I don't know what I am going to do.* Still, the people at Cook Children's were slowly becoming my second family. They didn't see me as "the cancer kid." They joked with me, laughed with me, and cried with me. They did their best to be there for me and to treat me like a normal kid.

I really didn't mind the MRI, the CAT scan, or the other exams. It was the bone scan that I dreaded, the reason being that it basically scans your entire body piece by piece, and it takes a really long time to do it. The scan could take up to an hour. They had to inject this dye stuff into my body so all the pretty colors would show up on the exam. It's a lot of fun, believe me. I'm sure everybody would love to be injected with dye and lie on a table as still as can be for what seems like forever. After a full day of these kinds of exams, I once again played the waiting game.

I prayed to God every night to look over me and to help me get through this journey. I prayed that the chemotherapy was working and that it was killing the tumor in my leg. I prayed that I would beat this thing. It was right around this time that I began to worry about things to the max. For that whole week until I got the results, I was a nervous wreck. I would plan out in my head what the results would be and how it was going to affect me. A big part of me wanted to believe that the chemotherapy was working. But another part of me was worried sick that the chemotherapy wasn't doing anything except make me feel like crap.

One day while I was up at the hospital receiving treatment, Dr. Murray came in to do his daily rounds. He told me that my results were back and that my tumor was getting smaller in size, all of which meant that the chemotherapy was working and doing its job. I remember this massive feeling of relief came over my entire body. It was the first sense of relief I'd had since I got diagnosed.

"What do we do now since the chemotherapy is working?' I asked him. "Am I almost done with all of this?"

"Surgery will be the next step," he said. "But while the tumor is smaller, it looks like it's starting to spread. There are two small spots right above your knee, and we need to think about surgery soon. We need to get those tumors out of your leg."

6

A DIFFICULT DECISION

This was the surgery I thought I was going to have *before* I got diagnosed. I just didn't think it would happen this way. Dr. Murray went on to tell me that after I had finished this latest round of chemo we would talk in detail more about surgery. Just like before, I wasn't scared of the fact that I would soon have to have surgery. I was ready to get this tumor out of my body for good. I swear, I would have gone that day and had the surgery. For once, my family and I saw some hope for my future. We were still scared about the possibilities, but this was good news—just enough for us to see a tiny little light at the end of a long tunnel. And a tiny light was all that we needed.

But when it came time to finish that round of chemo, I started to get anxious about the surgery. I wanted to get it over with and get back to my normal life. A few days following the last round of chemo, I had to go back up to the hospital for a checkup on my counts. My blood platelet count was low, so I had to receive another blood transfusion. Blood transfusions meant that I was probably going to be at the clinic all day.

Hours and hours went by, during which my mom and I were stuck in one of the exam rooms, watching a talk show and waiting for the transfusion to be complete. At some point Dr. Murray stuck his head in the room and said "Hey Scott, mind if I come in and talk to you guys for a second?"

When he entered the room, I had this sense that he was about to talk to me about something important and possibly scary. After seeing him week after week, I had started trying to read his body language and expressions in an attempt to tell if he was about to deliver good news or bad news. I judged his expression and began to prepare myself for bad news. I was now trying to find the strength to handle whatever came at me next. He began to explain that I had two options when it came to surgery.

He then began to describe what was called a "limb salvage surgery." He told us that they would cut open my leg, take out the tumor, take out bones that were infected with the tumor, and replace it all with a metal rod. The other option was amputation, meaning they would cut my leg off through the knee, or just a little bit above it.

He said that with the limb salvage surgery there was a small chance that they may not be able to get the entire tumor out, but with amputation, when the leg comes off, off goes the tumor with it. I was thinking to myself, *Which one are they leaning towards?* I never thought I would have to have me leg cut off. That was the last thing I wanted. *If they cut my leg off, how will I get back to playing sports?*

I explained to Dr. Murray that the whole motivation for wanting to beat this thing was to get back on the field. He got quiet for a minute, probably trying to find the right words to say what came next: "The reason I have told you about these two options is that I wanted you to have a say on what surgery you would want to go with. Either one is a big surgery and either one comes with results that you are going to have to live with for the rest of your life. You don't have to say anything now. You and your family can think about it and talk it over. I hate to ask you and your family to make such a huge decision, but given the circumstances these are your only two options."

I remember my mom and I both had these blank looks on our faces. We had just received the kind of news we never thought we would have to face. Dr. Murray went on to give me more details about each surgery. Apparently with the limb salvage operation, I was looking at more surgeries down the road because they would have to go into my other leg and work on the growth plates so I would be even in height. Most likely my mobility would be limited, and there was a chance that my body would reject the metal rod. And if I ever broke the metal rod, amputation would be the only option. The plus side was that I would keep my leg and live a relatively normal life.

With an amputation, the big minus was that I would lose half a leg and need to learn how walk with a prosthesis. He said I could jump out of a plane or do whatever with a prothesis; it was all on me. The way it was coming across to me was that with the limb salvage surgery I wouldn't be able to return to sports, but that with an amputation there was a possibility that I could be active again. As soon as that thought ran across my mind, I knew exactly what surgery I wanted. I didn't go and say it out loud at that moment because I didn't know how my parents were going to handle my decision.

Dr. Murray's suggestion was that I talk to a few people who had undergone these kinds of surgeries so that I could see how they live their lives; this would help me weigh my options. He had two people that he wanted me to meet. I asked if they were athletic, but he said no. I was a little bummed about that because I was hoping to meet an athlete, but I agreed to meet with both to see what they were like.

There I was, facing a huge, life-changing decision, and I was only fourteen years old. It was either one or the other, and a decision had to be made. When I thought about my passion for sports and wanting so badly to get back to an active lifestyle, the amputation would come to mind. When I thought about having the limb salvage surgery, I had this image of the doctors taking the tumor out and leaving a small piece in my leg, allowing the cancer to spread all over my body. As crazy as it sounds, amputation was becoming the choice for me.

But of course, nobody wants to lose a limb—especially not a teenage boy. I was trying to imagine my life with half my leg missing, and it was tough. I didn't know any amputees at the time. The only future I saw for myself was being active in sports. Not girls, not being social and how people would see me as an amputee, and not how hard it might be learn how to use a prosthesis. I just pictured myself getting back to sports and, some day, reaching my dream of becoming a professional athlete. That was all that mattered to me at the time.

On the way home, my mom spoke first. "Are you OK? Scott, I love you, and your dad and I will be behind you whatever decision you make," she said. All I could do was nod my head. I kept thinking this was just like the ride home after the diagnosis of cancer. I was hyper aware of everything going on around me as we made our way home. I saw people in their cars, at the gas station, going into a store. I couldn't help but wonder what kind of decisions they were making in their heads. Whatever it was, I knew it wasn't as huge as mine. I wished so much that I could just be normal. With the kinds of things I was going through and the decisions I was being asked to make, I felt the furthest thing from normal. Like I said, no one wants to lose a limb, but amputation felt like the right choice for me.

Later that week I got to meet a guy who had the same cancer as me and had opted for an amputation. Unfortunately for me, he was not at all athletic. I was trying to block that out of my head so that I would be prepared to hear everything he had to tell me. When he came walking towards me, the first thing I noticed was how he was walking. He'd worn shorts that day— I guess so that I could see his leg. I remember this metal object that was supposed to be his leg. He was explaining how his leg worked and how he was able to walk, but it was going right over my head. This was all new to me. I was trying to imagine myself with a leg like his, and it was tough. To him it seemed like no big deal. All in all, I was thankful to meet him and to have the opportunity to see what a prosthesis looked like and how it worked.

I was unable to actually meet someone with the limb salvage surgery, but I did get to catch a glimpse of a patient walking down the hall at the clinic who had had the limb salvage surgery. To me, he had a much bigger limp than the guy I had met with the amputation. I kept asking if there was anyone who'd had either surgery and was active. There was no one for me to meet, but I was given a video to view about amputees. I took it home, and my parents and I watched it. It was amazing to see people living such seemingly normal lives. One lady had lost her leg in an accident and now was a fashion model. She had a prosthesis that looked like an actual leg. Another guy had lost his leg to cancer and had been a survivor for years. He had a job, a family, and all the normal things in life.

There was one guy, though, who really caught my attention. He was younger than the others, probably in his twenties. I can't remember how he lost his leg, but he was saying how active he had been before his accident. Cut to the next scene and there he was playing half-court basketball with his friends. I'm sure a little grin came over my face at that point because that was exactly what I'd wanted to see. He wasn't the fastest or the most mobile on the court, but it was enough for me. I took it as a sign.

Amputation was my best option for sure and if I wanted to get back to sports, this was the surgery for me. There wasn't much talking during the video. I would look over to my parents every now and then and try to read their facial expressions. I could tell that the thought of their own son losing his leg was more than they could handle. My parents were still on the fence about my decision, but they didn't want to come out and tell me what to do.

Later that night I went into my parent's room to talk to my mom. I was dying to know what my parents' thoughts were on my decision, so I asked my mom to just come out and tell me what she wanted me to do. Of course, she said the same thing she'd been saying since this all started: they were behind me no matter what decision I made. "You are the one that is going to have to live with it for the rest of your life, Scott," she said. "We will back you and support you whatever you decide to do."

I still had to know which way she was leaning. I knew for sure my dad did not want me to have the amputation. He had mentioned that he wanted to do everything possible to save my leg. As for my mom, I didn't know. I came up with an idea and brought it to her. "I'll write my decision on a piece of paper, and you write what you think I should do on another piece of paper. Then we can reveal our answers to each other at the same time," I explained. Seeing how much this was bothering me, she agreed to do it. Knowing what I wanted to do, I wrote down *amputation*. I saw my mom take a few seconds as if to think it over, and then she wrote her decision down. She gave a big sigh and turned to face me. I asked my mom to reveal her decision first. When her paper was turned over, it read *save your leg*.

I gave a slight nod and a meager smile to my mom, who was trying to fight back the tears. Now I knew that both of my parents were hoping I would decide to save my leg. I was a bit hesitant to reveal my decision, knowing that it was different from my parents. I slowly unfolded my paper and revealed the word *amputation* to my mom. I could see my mom's eyes tear up some more.

I quickly began to explain: "Mom, I'm scared if I have the other surgery that they'll leave a small piece of cancer in my leg, and it will come back and be worse. If I have the amputation, I feel like I have a better chance of staying alive. The way I see it, it's either save my leg or save my life." With that last statement, I saw that it finally hit home for my mother that my life was more important than how I would look physically. She nodded, stepping forward to fold me into a hug. "We'll support you no matter what," she whispered into my ear.

DECISION MADE

So from that point, it was set. I was to have the amputation. I did feel a little better about it once I knew that my parents understood the reasons behind my decision. The next day, I told Dr. Murray that I wanted to have the amputation as my surgery. It was scheduled for a couple of weeks away.

Still having my regular, and brutal, chemotherapy treatments, I was scheduled to have another MRI to check the status of my tumor. This being my third MRI in the past couple months, it had become routine for me. There I would lie, with my headphones on listening to music, as still as I could for a good thirty to forty minutes. As with most of my tests in the past, I didn't get the results that day. All I could do was hope and pray that the chemo was working and killing the tumor. A few days later, I was at the clinic again for a checkup on my blood counts when Dr. G came into the room. At this point we really didn't like to see her because it seemed she always brought bad news. She was the one that told me flat out that I had cancer and she had been very much straight to the point about it. She never beat around the bush and never sugar-coated anything for me. Sometimes her style was really hard to handle, especially with what I had already been through. So here she was, telling us that amputation was now my only option. She told us that there were now two more tumor spots that had showed up on my latest MRI.

You have got to be kidding me. It's getting smaller but it's spreading? I was beginning to think that che-motherapy just wasn't working for me. The two new spots had appeared high up on my femur close to my hip bone. So now instead of an amputation through the knee or right above the knee, my only option was for them to take my entire leg. She went on to tell us that they needed to do this as soon as possible before it spread to my lungs. With a leg amputated at the hip, sports were out of the question. She also told us that I needed to have a biopsy first thing in the morning to make sure that these were cancerous tumors.

I felt like I was reliving the diagnosis day all over again. Dr. G told us that since the tumor seemed to be spreading at a fast pace, she was now uncertain that the chemo was actually working. This meant that my chances for survival were diminishing. Being told that the hell I had suffered through for the past two months may not have been working vaulted me over the edge. I got this feeling that my days were numbered and that the cancer was quickly killing me.

We all begin to cry. We held on to each other, each of us gripped by fear. My mom asked the doctor if she would kindly step out of the room so that we could have a minute to ourselves. All we did was cry and cry. It was as if we all knew that I wasn't going to make it. I was losing this battle, yet we still held on to what little faith we had that there might still be a chance. My parents told me they would do whatever they had to do for me.

I was trying to picture myself without a leg and wondering how functional I would be. It broke my heart all over again that it meant sports were out of the question. I was slowly being beaten down by this emotional roller coaster I was being forced to ride. I wasn't sure how much more I could take. It definitely felt like Death was in the room—and it was coming for me.

The next day we arrived at Cook Children's for the biopsy. I was at the point where I just wanted them to go ahead and cut my leg off. I was so emotionally and physically drained that I didn't think I had any fight left in me. Before I was wheeled back to the operating room, my mom and family came by my bed to kiss me and tell me that they loved me. They told me that they would be praying for me and that I was going to be OK. My dad, on his way to the hospital from work, wasn't able to get there before I was taken back.

When I was finally wheeled off, the anesthesia was taking its effect, and I was getting drowsy. Before I knew it, I was knocked out cold.

I found out later that not ten minutes after they wheeled me into surgery, my mom saw Dr. G walking towards her holding an MRI scan. My mom was overcome with fear about what the doctor was going to tell her. She was imagining that the doctor was going to tell her that they had discovered tumors all over my body and that it was worse than they had thought. Apparently the first words out of Dr. G's mouth were "I'm sorry. I'm sorry." At that point, my mom really started to lose it, because she thought that they had lost me when I was on the table.

My mom was in a state of shock and, not being able to fully understand what Dr. G was trying to explain to her, could only stare at her. Dr. G saw this and said flat out, "We had the MRI upside down." My mom was being told that when they read the MRI, they were reading it upside down and had been looking at the two same spots that were on *top* of my knee. There were no spots on my hip. My mom just started to cry and laugh, all at the same time. She was so grateful she couldn't even get mad at Dr. G. In fact, she ended up giving the doctor a big hug and thanking her for finding the mistake. At this point my dad had arrived to see my mother hugging the doctor. He was confused about what was going on and asked them what was happening.

"They had the MRI upside down. Scott doesn't have cancer on his hip," my mom told my dad. He didn't take the news as well as my mother had; he was furious.

"He has already been through so much! Do you have any idea what the news did to us?" demanded my dad. Dr. G could only apologize again.

But for me, I had to wait until I awoke from surgery to get the news. As I came to, I saw Dr. G standing over me, trying to talk to me. I remember that it was hard to make out what she was saying. I looked over to my right and saw my mom in the distance. I rose up slightly and asked her to come closer. I saw tears in her eyes and automatically began to fear the worst. "You don't have cancer on your hip, Scott. They had the MRI upside down. It hasn't spread!" my mom told me. I lowered my head back down to the pillow and stared up at the ceiling. I couldn't decide whether I was mad or upset or happy. I welled up. I almost couldn't believe it. Eventually, when the shock wore off, I realized all I was feeling was thankful and blessed.

The doctor apologized and said I could take a week off and wait to have the surgery since I had just managed to get off one heck of an emotional roller coaster. I declined and said I wanted the surgery as soon as possible. I was incredibly grateful that I didn't have tumors on my hip, but I was still fearful the cancer would spread if I waited any longer, and I didn't want to take that chance. I wanted my leg off as soon as possible. I didn't want to go through anything like this ever again.

A few days later I was at the hospital to have my amputation. That whole morning, I was thinking to myself, *This is the last time I will walk to the bathroom; this is the last time I will put my shoe on this foot; this is the last time I will walk down a set of steps on both my feet.* It was an indescribable feeling. Believe it or not, it was a surgery I was ready to have. My family, a few close friends, and I were all together, waiting for them to take me back for my surgery. Finally the time came for me to be wheeled to the operating room. Everyone lined up and, one by one, wished me luck. Although this was a big surgery, I wasn't scared. I believed that once the leg was gone, I would be cancer-free.

As they wheeled me off, my mother slipped something into my hand. It was a tiny piece of paper, and on it she had written:

> *I said a prayer for you today, and I know God must have heard. I felt the answer in my heart although he spoke no words. I didn't ask for wealth or fame. I knew you wouldn't mind. I asked him to send treasures of a far more lasting kind. I asked that he be near you at the start of each new day and to grant you health and blessings and friends to share your way. I asked for happiness for you in all things, great and small. But it was for his loving care I prayed the most of all.*

As I finished reading, the drugs kicked in, and I began to feel drowsy. I heard loud music and the staff singing along to a country song. I thought to myself, *These guys are sure having a good time, considering they are about to cut my leg off.* I was asked what flavor I wanted for the mask that would be placed over me to help put sleep. I chose bubble gum. As they placed the mask over my mouth and nose, I counted backwards from one hundred.

"100, 99, 98 . . . ."

I was out cold.

It's customary during these kinds of surgeries that the family is kept up-to-date by phone calls from the operating room. About three hours into my surgery, the phone rang in the waiting room, and my mom picked it up. "Mrs. Odom, his leg is off," said the voice on the other end of the line. Hearing this, my mother hung up the phone and began walking slowly around the room with her head down, not saying a word. Everyone in the room fell silent. They knew, without being told, that the message had been 'his leg is off.' Hours went by, and the room remained silent. Finally, at the six-hour mark, the last phone call was placed, letting my family know that the surgery was complete. I was not only a cancer patient; I was an above-the-knee amputee at the age of fourteen.

8

PHANTOM PAIN

They would only allow one person at a time into the recovery room. I was slowly coming to and seemingly felt no pain; the feeling was more like my leg had fallen asleep. I saw my mom and the nurses standing over me. I tried to find the strength to get out a few words, but it was a battle. Finally, I managed to croak, "Did they cut my leg off? I feel the same." I guess I expected to be in pain or something. The nurses told me that my leg was off, but I was having a hard time believing them. They carefully pulled back the covers, showing me the bandages and wraps on what was left of my leg. With what little strength I had, I lifted my head and looked down. I saw no right foot. All I could see was a huge bandage wrapped around my thigh. Thanks to the morphine pump, I dozed off.

That whole day, I remained knocked out. The next day I was slowly waking, little by little. I was told I might experience a thing called "phantom pain" and that even though my leg was gone, there was a chance that I could still feel pain in it. They told me some amputees get it and some don't. For those who do get it, the sensation can range from mild to unbearable. Fortunately for me, I had no pain. It still felt like my leg and my foot were still attached to my body; the only difference was that they felt like they'd fallen asleep. My parents, anxious to see my leg, pulled back the covers. I think they were relieved that it wasn't as bad as they had originally thought. I guess they were expecting something gruesome, like a bloody bandage. I could see that they were slowly accepting that this was my new reality.

Later that same day, a physical therapist came by to work with me. By that time I was feeling pretty alert. The therapist was a nice young lady by the name of Carla. I came to learn that she always had a big smile on her face. It was comforting to see.

Since I had been lying in bed for almost a day and a half, she asked me if I would be alright with sitting on the side of the bed. A little nervous about the idea because I didn't want anything to get pulled out of me, I agreed. I was also wondering how I would be able to sit with half my leg missing. Very slowly she helped me, and as I sat up, I got a little dizzy. After sitting there for a few minutes, Carla asked me how I was feeling.

"I feel pretty good. Not too bad," I answered.

"You think you're up for standing?" she asked.

"I could try, I guess," I replied. I was ready to get this show on the road. She explained how we were going to do this, and I took in as much as I could. Carla then put a gait belt around me in case I lost my balance. A gait belt is a device used to transfer a patient from one position to another. It's made out of cotton webbing and has a metal buckle on one end. The idea is that it puts less strain on the back of the therapist and provides support for the patient. Putting a walker in front of me, she told me I was to push off from the bed with my hands. When my bottom was off the bed, I was to grab the walker for support. I sat there for a minute, thinking it over while I tried to calm my nerves. I knew this was part of the long road to recovery and that it had to be done.

Slowly, and with a little help from Carla, I stood up on my one and only leg. As I stood, I could feel all the blood start to rush down to what was now my stump. It was a weird feeling and a little uncomfortable. I stood there for about a minute before asking if I could sit back down. I rested for a few minutes. "Do you think you can try it again?" asked Carla. "You are doing so awesome, Scott." I nodded my head. I stood up with little effort without as much discomfort as the last time.

"Do you think you can take a few steps?" she asked. *Steps,* I thought. *Is she blind? I only have one leg.* She explained how I would begin to learn to take a step with my leg. I was to move my walker a little bit in front of me and, putting weight onto my arms, I would take a small step with my leg. She made it sound so easy. Doing as she explained to me, I took my first step. It wasn't as bad or as hard as I thought it would be. I told her I could do more, if she wanted me to. With a big smile on her face, she opened my room door and told me I could go as far as I was able to. The first step became the second, and then the third, and then the fourth, and so on. Before I knew it, I was halfway around the nurses' station. I ended up doing a full lap or so around the floor before it was all said and done. I not only impressed myself, but everybody else, too. I could tell that seeing me walk down the hall gave my parents a huge sense of relief.

A few days went by, and it was time for me to leave the hospital. I had been doing my physical therapy and was at a point where they could begin to wean me off of the pain medication. The last thing for them to do was to remove my catheter. A female nurse came into the room and said that she was going to take it out for me.

Now for those of you who don't know what a catheter is, it's a tube about the width of a dime. On a male patient, it's inserted into their urethra. I have no idea how the *heck* they got that in there because I'd been blissfully unaware and under sedation at the time. But now, I was very much awake. So I was very nervous about how, exactly, it was coming out. And, of course, they had to tape some of the tube to my thigh so it wouldn't get accidentally pulled out. Pulling the tape off was a pain in and of itself—it seemed as if my skin came with it as she was slowly pulled the tape off.

While she is doing this, I had my mom hold a sheet between the nurse and myself. For one, I didn't want to see what she was doing and for another, I didn't want my mom to see my business. The nurse finally got the tape off my thigh and looked back at me. "Do you want me to count to three or just pull it out?" she asked.

"Wait. Wait!" I told her in a panic. I was *not* prepared for this and was dreading the pain I was about to experience. After a few minutes, I mumbled, "OK, count to three."

"One, two, three," she counted. On three, she pulled. It was the worst pain I have ever experienced—and I'd just had most of my right leg removed. I let out the biggest scream of my life. I'm sure people within a ten-mile radius heard me. It felt like she was pulling a water hose out of my penis, and the water hose was a mile long. Just when I thought it was over, she was still pulling more tube out. When it finally ended I could not believe what had just taken place. I lay there in agony, thankful that it was over. Never again will I have one of those things inserted in me. I wouldn't wish that on my worst enemy.

I didn't want any more of that stuff. If I was to have any more surgeries, I would rather pee all over myself than to have another catheter; and I let that be known. A few hours later, the nurse came back in and gave my parents the discharge information that another nurse was going to come to the house for the first week or so to take care of me and to teach my mom how to change my bandages and wrap my stump. I was to take about two weeks off before I was to start another round of chemotherapy. They wanted to give my body a break from everything that had taken place in the past two months. I had taken a good amount of chemotherapy, and on top of that I had just undergone an amputation. I thought I deserved a break. It was the protocol of my diagnosis that I was to receive more chemotherapy after surgery to ensure there wasn't a small piece of cancer that neither X-rays nor MRIs could detect. It was to be better safe than sorry.

When the nurse came out that first day back home, it would be the first time I was to see my stump. I was anxious and nervous. The nurse carefully took the tape off from around the bandage and then slowly began to unwrap it. When all of the bandages were off, there was still a wet yellow strip of material over the bottom of my stump. I kept asking her if any of this was going to hurt, and she kept telling me it wouldn't.

As she began to remove the yellow strip, what was now my "leg" was revealed. My stump did not have stitches, as I had expected. It did have staples—thirty-two of them, to be precise. It was hard at first to take it all in because it wasn't what I had been expecting. It was sick-looking and a little scary. It reminded me of the Frankenstein monster's forehead.

The staples were huge and went from the left side of my leg all the way around to the right. It looked painful, but it wasn't. The nurse then began to gently clean my leg, demonstrating for my mother how it should be done each day to ensure that my stump didn't get infected. She then taught her the figure-eight wrapping of the bandage to cover my stump.

For the next two weeks, I did nothing but rest and sleep. If I had pain, it was very little. I had still not experienced any phantom pain. I would look down every now and then and just stare at what was left of my leg. It had been cut off just a few inches above the knee.

At the time, my parents were concerned that, given how my stump looked, I would come to regret the surgery. But I didn't regret it because I had this enormous sense of relief that the cancer was gone, cut out of me for good. I did feel very dependent, though, on my family. I wasn't able to fully take a bath; I had to be given a sponge bath, and if I needed something I had to call on them. I didn't like the feeling of helplessness it gave me, but I knew I also didn't have a choice. If I did get around on my own, it was in a wheelchair. I hated staying indoors for long periods at a time, so I would wheel myself outside and shoot some hoops in my backyard. While on the court, I began to feel like myself again. Even though I was in a wheelchair and had just had my leg amputated, shooting hoops seemed to take that all away.

9

SETBACKS

My two-week hiatus came to an end and I was due back at Cook Children's for more chemotherapy. It was around this time that I began to feel moody and emotional because I didn't understand why I had to keep going back for more chemotherapy. Hadn't I just given my leg to cancer? With all the chemo I'd taken in the past two months, my body had changed dramatically. I was weak and slow-moving. I felt like an old man.

Dr. Murray explained to me that the type of cancer I had normally goes to the lungs, making the extra rounds of chemo a necessity. Luckily for me, my lungs looked clear; no cancer had shown up in any of the test results. But according to the protocol, I was due for six more months of chemotherapy treatments to make sure there wasn't any cancer in my lungs. He called these six months of treatment the 'clean-up crew.' Not questioning him, I did as I was told.

Even with it being called the clean-up crew, he said we still had to be aggressive in the treatment, so I was still taking the hardest chemotherapy drugs. The first round back was rough because it knocked me back down again. Throwing up several times a day and not eating took its toll.

Nurses were constantly coming into my room checking my urine and vital signs. Even if it was at two in the morning, and I was sound asleep, I would be awakened by the squeezing of my arm by a blood pressure cuff. It was very irritating and I never got used to it.

My senses were still messed up and any kind of smell might set me off. It was just like before; anybody with strong perfume or food was not allowed in my room. I couldn't handle it. I ended up putting a sign on my door for the cafeteria people to please not bring the food tray into my room. I would be sound asleep and they would quietly bring my food tray and set it down on the table in front of my bed. Unfortunately, the smell would pull me, instantly sick to my stomach, from sleep and I'd need a bucket.

This was my life. This was my everyday. Since I stayed sick and weak most of the time, I was given a wheelchair to get from place to place. The few times I felt well enough, I preferred to use crutches instead of the walker.

As the weeks went by, I became anxious and eager to start the process of getting fitted for a prosthetic limb. I was eventually told by my doctors that my blood counts were high enough that I could venture out and find a place I liked that would fit me for a prosthesis.

I didn't want to be out in public because I was very self-conscious about how I looked. I felt like once I got fitted for a new leg, I would feel more normal and could get back to my life. We asked the social workers at the hospital if we could get the names and information for a number of prosthetic companies nearby so I could begin the process.

I wanted to go to a place that would believe in me and try to get me back to my goal of playing sports. The first place we went to was in a building down the street from Cook Children's. I was excited and eager to see what my leg would look like. When I got called back to the room, I was greeted by an older man. He asked me, "What are looking to get back to doing?" I told him that I was very eager to begin walking and getting back to playing baseball and basketball.

He was quiet for a moment and then said something truly devastating. "Well, son, with your level of amputation—that being one above the knee—I find it very hard and almost impossible to believe that you can get back to those sports." I looked at him with anger and disgust. I didn't want someone to make me a leg who didn't believe in me. I quickly turned my head away.

"You have no idea what he's capable of," my mother told him. We left his office before he could say anything else. I was very discouraged. *Was it going to be like this at the other offices?*

But even then I had the drive and determination that no matter what people said, I was going to do what I wanted to do. The next prosthetic clinic was a few streets down and was called Nova Care. It had a much bigger office and there were actual amputees in the waiting room. While my parents were filling out paperwork, I was observing the amputees in the office walking back and forth; I was paying attention to how they got around. Most of them were older men but it was interesting to see how they used their legs. It seemed like it was a part of them, as though it wasn't giving them any trouble. It seemed to work like a normal leg, but it was metal.

This time I was greeted by a younger man. He introduced himself to me and to my parents before taking us back to a big room with parallel bars running around the perimeter. It also had pictures on the wall of amputees doing all kind of activities: amputees skiing, riding bikes, and hard at work. I was feeling better about this place.

The guy began by asking me the same questions I was asked at the previous office. When we came around to the question of my goals, I told him, flat out: *sports.* "I want to play baseball and basketball again," I said. "Is that all?" he asked. "If that's what you want, I'll do everything I can to fit you with a leg that'll give you the opportunity to do so," he told me.

My mom still had her reservations and told him about the man at the other place and how she wondered if my expectations were realistic. "It won't be easy, but as long as he wants to do it, and he works hard at it, he can do whatever he wants to do," he told us.

I was so relieved. I knew, finally, that I was in the right place. *This* was the place that was going to help me get back to sports. After we talked for a while, he brought out some knees and feet, showing me what he thought would be good for me. Seeing the components of the leg was interesting and I was excited about getting started. He told me my next step was to get fitted for a socket to wear.

The socket is what my actual stump, or leg, would go into. This would allow me to move the prosthesis. But before any of that could happen, I needed to finish the chemotherapy treatments. Chemotherapy appointments meant that it was hard for me to go to the prosthetic clinic on a regular basis. And, when I was off of treatments, I had to make sure that my blood counts were up before I could do anything at all. I also needed to get my staples out and be cleared by my doctors to get fitted.

Regardless, I felt hopeful. I had this strong conviction that that once I got the process of getting my prosthetic going, I would be up and walking in no time and back to playing sports. Boy, was I wrong.

Even though my life had changed dramatically in such a short period of time, I never managed to get used to being restricted. For the most part, during my treatment, visitors were limited. One reason was because I was sick the majority of the time and another was because my counts were so low. If my counts where low, I really couldn't be around anybody. As the days went by, they were getting longer and longer. I was used to being outside, playing, being active. Now, the only thing I had to entertain myself was video games and TV talk shows.

Some days were harder than others. My friends came around less often and I was beginning to feel socially isolated—not a part of any social clique. I couldn't go out in public because of my counts. At the same time, I wouldn't have wanted to go outside because of how I looked: skinny, bald, pale as a ghost, and missing half my leg. My self-confidence had dropped dramatically and I was terrified of being seen in public.

I did go out with my parents. We went to Walmart when they begged me to go with them. I figured I would give it a try. When we arrived at the parking lot, butterflies overcame my stomach and I started to get nervous. My dad got the wheelchair out of the back of the car and brought it over to me. I got in the chair and he wheeled me to the front doors. As we got closer, I had my head dropped, feeling as though people were staring at me. We entered the store. It was loud. I slowly raised my head. I felt like all eyes were on me. We were passing little kids and older people, and they were staring and pointing. I had tried to prepare myself for this, but to be in that situation . . . I hated it. I asked my parents to take me back to the car. I was holding the tears back out of embarrassment. When we finally got back in the car, I broke down. I couldn't even go to the store with my parents without feeling disgusted; without having people stare and point at me. My dad headed back to the store, and my mom stayed in the car with me. I was overwhelmed by how hard it been to go out in public.

My weight was the lowest it had ever been: ninety-five pounds. I avoided mirrors because I didn't like the way I looked. The few times I did catch myself in the mirror, I would just stare for a few minutes and then begin to cry. Don't get me wrong, I was thankful to be alive. But at the same time, I was now fighting to accept who I had become: a shell of my former self.

I felt like a circus freak, like I should be in a cage so paying customers could walk by and stare at me. To make matters worse, the whole time I was thinking about girls. I mean, I was fourteen after all. I couldn't help but think, *Why would any girl want to be with me?* and *What girl would want a boyfriend with one leg?* I was trying to accept the fact that even though I never got to experience the girlfriend thing, it was now out of the question for me. No matter how much I thought a girl was cute, I had no chance, and I wouldn't take the chance because of how I felt.

I was also feeling that my body wasn't mine. I had this huge port in my upper chest. I had no hair anywhere on my body and my leg had been cut off above the knee. I could see my ribs jutting out and I had no strength. I cried myself to sleep many nights.

I felt like my body had been to hell and back. I would dream of the day I was to have my last chemo treatment. No more coming to the hospital on a regular basis, no more getting sick several times a day, no more pain, and no more boredom. This battle I was waging was the hardest thing I would ever have to go through, and I was scared and fearful of what each new day would bring. I thought about how much I was missing out on friends, school, and sports. I would just lie there and cry and cry, sometimes for hours at a time. I didn't know why this was happening to me. I was depressed. Even though I knew I was becoming depressed, I tried never to get upset around my parents.

I knew if I started crying, they would follow. I loved them and needed them more than anything. The worst times were when we would return home from a chemo treatment. My mom was instructed to continually check my temperature; if it was high, we were under strict orders to return to the hospital. I was getting to the point where I would beg my mom to not take it. But being the good mother that she is, my temperature was checked regularly.

About eight times out of ten, I had a fever. I would be home for a few hours, check my temperature, and then head right back to the hospital to stay for a few more days. This really got to me. I'd get so upset and angry because I felt like I had no control over my life. I lived in a hospital, not in a house. I was very moody—not because I chose to be, but because of the things I had to go through on a daily basis. I was so emotionally drained that I didn't even know how I was going to feel from one day to the next. I often felt trapped in a bad dream, with no way out.

A week or so went by and it was time to take the staples out of my leg. Just by the sound of it, it was going to hurt, so I was trying to mentally prepare myself. I'd had to wait a little longer than normal to get them out because my counts had been low. Dr. G came into the room.

"Hey Scott, you ready to get those staples out?" she asked.

I can't wait, it's going to be so much fun, I thought. "I guess so," I said. I got up on the table and lay on my back, staring up at the ceiling, holding my mother's hand for support.

Now, the bad thing about waiting a little longer to get the staples out was that some skin had started to grow over the staples. They had made themselves more than comfortable in my stump. Some of them the doctor could pull out with little effort, but others *really* hurt. At times she had to really *dig*. I'm sure the people from across the street could hear me.

Tears just rolled down the side of my face, I looked up at my mom and she, too, was crying. To see her son in pain, and there was nothing she could do about it, was really hard to watch. The thirty-two staples the doctor pulled out felt more like *one hundred* and thirty. Finally, the last one was out and it was over. I lay there, trying to get myself together. It was nowhere near the catheter, but still—not fun.

A few days later, I was cleared to go back to Nova Care. My spirits were up. I was getting my leg. The first step was to make a cast of my stump and build a socket from it. I sat in a chair, my mom at my side, and watched the guy getting everything prepared to make the cast. He put a large sheet of brown paper on the floor, filled a bucket with water, and got out a bunch of measuring tools. I had to strip down to my underwear and put some kind of panty hose on over my stump. At this time, my stump still didn't look normal. What it looked like was the boney end of your elbow. I was continuing to lose weight and it showed. He told me to stand up and hold onto the parallel bars for balance. He plunged a crusty white bandage into the water and quickly began to wrap my leg. Making sure to get a good fit, he was pushing into me to make it tighter. Seconds went by, and the bandage began to dry and get hard. Finally, after several more bandages, he carefully began to pull the mold off of my leg.

I was told I would have to come back later in the week for what was known as a "test socket." This would be a hard plastic fitting that would determine whether or not the mold he made for my leg was a good fit. Although it doesn't seem like a lot, it was very time consuming. Days went by before I could return to the clinic for my test socket fitting. The end of my stump was looking worse and beginning to feel sore. You could pretty much see, and feel, the bone at the end.

The prosthetist seeing this, put some pads at the end of the test socket so I could avoid placing all of my weight on the end of my leg. When I tried the test socket for the first time it was very uncomfortable. I had this plastic thing riding high on my hip and pinching some of my business. Already sore and scared to put full weight on my leg, I held onto the bars as tight as I could. At the end of the socket was not a prosthetic knee and foot, but a straight metal pole with a rubber stopper on the end of it. It looked nothing like a leg.

I was told this was only for the fitting and nothing more. I wasn't going to try to walk that day. The fitting was a bit off and did not feel the best. I was told if I were to lose or gain just five pounds it would mess up the fitting, and since I was on chemo, my weight was never the same. I had to do yet another fitting. I was getting discouraged. Getting a leg was turning out to be a long and frustrating process. Also, my stump was very sore. I could still feel the ridges from the surgical knife they'd used to cut off my leg.

I was soon back at Cook Children's for a check-up on my blood work and more tests. While there, they looked over my stump and didn't like the way it looked either. The red and purple flesh at the end of my stump concerned them. They decided that I was to stop going to Nova Care until I finished my chemo treatments. They told me that the fluctuations in my weight from the chemo made getting properly fitted for a prosthesis impossible anyway.

Soon after, I was told why I had the redness at the end of my stump: I had a staph infection in my leg. The plan of attack was to put me on medication and then go back into my leg and cut another inch or so off my stump. Surprisingly, I didn't mind having the surgery because my leg was hurting so bad; I just wanted it fixed. The only way I would agree to the surgery was if they promised to not place a catheter in me. They told me this kind of surgery didn't require one. *Praise God.* How funny is that? There I was getting even more cut off of my leg and all I was worried about was the catheter.

A week or so later, when my counts were good, I had the surgery. I got to go home the next day. This time, when we took the bandage off, my stump was fatty. No staples either, just some stitches. It looked a lot better and wasn't nearly as painful. The hardest thing was that I'd have to wait months before I could get fitted for my prosthesis.

HOPE FOR THE FUTURE

After the second big surgery, it was back to life at Cook Children's. I was up there every other week to have my chemo treatments and checkups. I was even more moody and depressed. I felt like it was never going to end and I was going to have to do this for the rest of my life just to stay alive. I wondered what my leg was going to look like and dreamed of getting back on the field as if I'd never missed a step. Going through the aggressive chemo left me with fevers and nose bleeds. They told me that while the chemo was working, it was also killing everything inside me.

We got the test results back from my amputation. After the second surgery they'd sent some tissue from my stump to pathology. Finally, some good news. The chemo had killed ninety-eight percent of the tumor in my knee. Hearing the news, I felt so relieved. Even though my body was going through hell, we were finally getting somewhere with this disease. Even though I felt and looked like crap, I was actually getting better. The more fevers I got, the more Dr. Murray looked into them. He finally came to the conclusion that I had what he called "tumor fever." It was the best kind of fever you could get in those circumstances. When he told me this, I tried to take it as a good sign.

Being in the hospital so much, it began to feel like home and the nurses began to feel like family. They treated me like a normal kid, laughed and joked with me, and gave me their time and attention. I know this did a ton for my recovery. In fact, the whole staff at the hospital was a special group of people. They gave me hope for the future, even when it was hard for me to see it. There was no other place I would rather have been to fight this thing. I felt as though God had put me in that hospital for a reason and the people working there were the best of the best. They were His angels, sent from heaven to take care of me. It's hard to put into words the care and support I got at Cook Children's. I had put all of my trust in them, and I knew they would do anything and everything to help me.

And by anything, I mean *anything!* One time, after a week-long chemo treatment, I was back home recovering. While watching TV in my room, my nose began to itch. I absently scratched it and the next thing I knew I was staring down at bed sheets splattered in blood. I hopped in my wheelchair and headed for the bathroom. Minutes passed and the toilet began to pile up with bloody tissues. My mom found me in the bathroom and, seeing the mound of bloody tissue paper, got on the phone with the hematology clinic. They told my mom to take me back to the hospital. I spent the thirty-minute drive with my head back, going through a ton of tissues. We finally arrived at the clinic and were brought back to a room with three female nurses in it. They tried tilting my head back but it just made me cough up clots of blood. Then one of the nurses got an idea. She grabbed a small, tube-like thing from one of the cabinets. Then she told me that she was going to stick it up my nose as far as it could go, and the foam inside the tube would expand in my nostril, stopping the blood flow. I looked over at my mom and she was trying desperately not to laugh. When the nurses saw her, they too began to laugh. "What is so funny?" I asked, laughing a little myself even though I had no idea what was so funny.

"Do you know what you have up your nose right now?" asked my mom. I shook my head. "Son," said my mother, really laughing now. "You have a tampon up your nose." My face got bright red. All I could do was smile and shake my head. We were all laughing. As funny and as mortifying as it was, it had really worked. That tampon cured my nosebleed.

Humor was a real lifesaver and helped me get through the tough times. I had to laugh at myself. I didn't have a choice. As a family, we were always trying to find a way to laugh it off. I believe laughter is the best medicine and it helped me look at the brighter side of life.

Two guys from Joshua High School really brought that laughter to me. These were two guys I didn't know before my diagnosis, but when they heard I was sick they were eager to meet me. They were the type of guys who just wanted to help. I agreed to meet them because it was getting pretty lonely at the hospital. Don't get me wrong—I love my parents and brother—but I was ready to socialize with other people. Nick and Kyle were their names and they were seniors. When they came and visited with me, I felt normal again. Even though these guys didn't really know me yet, they treated me like I had been their friend for years. We would share stories and laugh the entire time we were together. I was in much better spirits and fortunate to have their company. It was a huge boost for me. Even though it wasn't on a regular basis, I was still grateful whenever they stopped by to see me. I don't think people realize how much it means to have someone visit with you during cancer treatment. It is amazing how much of an effect it can have on you, knowing that you have people who are pulling for you.

During this time I also got the opportunity to meet some famous athletes. I got to meet guys from the Dallas Cowboys and the Texas Rangers. Out of all the folks I got to meet, there were just a handful that were actually there to meet me and showed an interest. Don't get me wrong, I was excited to meet everyone. After all, I'm a huge sports fan. But, even though I was thankful, it was a disappointing experience when I met an athlete that seemed like they didn't want to be there with me.

Thank goodness for Troy Aikman, Daryl Johnston, Hershel Walker, and Scott Murray. For those who don't know his name, Scott Murray was a sportscaster who was at that time with *NBC 5* in Dallas. These guys were great. I was able to have actual conversations with them. It was like they were more excited to meet me than I was to meet them. One night, after having a grueling chemo treatment, I heard that Scott Murray was down in the lobby giving a speech. The nurses were trying their best to see if they could get him to come up to my room and visit with me and, before I knew it, he was walking through my hospital room door. Right off the bat, we began to talk sports. He asked me who my favorite athletes were. He was very interested to hear about my dream of getting back to sports. During that time, I just happened to look over at the clock and a half hour had already passed by. Before he left, he asked me if I would be interested in coming to Dallas to watch a taping of the *Daryl Johnston Show*. I was very excited at the idea, but I have to admit that at the time I thought he was just talk. *Would I really get a chance to sit in on a taping of the show?* When he left, he and my parents exchanged numbers. I was on cloud nine. Just to be able to sit and talk sports with someone who talked sports for a living . . . amazing! He showed so much interest in my goal of getting back to sports; I was really touched.

Two days later, my mom got a call. It was Scott
Murray and he wanted to know if we could make it
down the next night to see a taping. He was going
to meet us and then we were going to follow him to
the studio. This was very exciting. One: I was going
to meet Daryl Johnston and two: I was going to get
a behind-the-scenes peek at all the action. When we
arrived at the studio, Scott asked us to wait a few minutes before taking us back to the set. When he came
back, he was holding all kinds of sports memorabilia.
When we had met that first night, I'd mentioned to
him that I was a big Barry Sanders fan. He'd remem-
bered and he had all this Barry Sanders sports memorabilia for me. I was the happiest kid on earth. It
was a great experience to sit and watch a taping of an
actual sports show. That drive to get back to playing
sports had been reignited. The special guest on the
show that day was former Dallas Cowboys running
back, Herschel Walker. I was in awe to see him in person. After the taping, the people watching with us got
out of their seats and tried to get Herschel Walker's
attention so they could get an autograph. Politely ex-
cusing himself, he walked right past them and right
up to me. He introduced himself to us and I'm pretty
sure my face said it all. He was the friendliest person
I had ever met. He chatted with us for a little while,
signed some autographs for me, and even took some
pictures with us.

Meeting my idols really helped me get through
those tough times. It helped get my mind off of things.
Especially because, at the time, I felt like I had to be

this strong kid to get through it all and beat the cancer. But being the strong kid was exhausting. Truth be told, I was having more bad days than good. That day, though, was one for the books for me.

CAMP SANGUINITY

As the summer of '98 approached, Jill Koss, director of child life at Cook Children's, approached me about a new opportunity. I was asked if I would like to go to a week-long camp for kids with cancer and blood disorders. It was called Camp Sanguinity. I was adamantly against the idea. I was not comfortable with the way I looked. Besides, I wasn't going to know anybody. They understood my reservations, but at the same time they thought this might help and be a good experience for me. The camp was a month away and I was told I could think about it. If I changed my mind, they would be glad to have me.

The camp offer came up time after time and even my mom wanted me to go. I was brought a video so I could see what went on at the camp. It showed kids swimming, riding horses, doing archery, climbing a rope course, fishing, and even playing in the mud. It all looked like a lot of fun but I still wasn't convinced. I didn't have my leg yet and I just wasn't comfortable being out in public. I was very lonely at this time because I wasn't getting many visitors.

I began to wonder if God wasn't trying to tell me something. Due to all that I'd been through, my relationship to God was closer than ever. I prayed to Him and I put my life in His hands. I began to see another side to this whole camp thing: I was still nervous and scared but I was also starting to feel that I should give it a try. It wasn't until the day before camp began that I decided to go. Another thing that convinced me was finding out that the camp had a basketball court. It was kind of nice to think that for a whole week I wasn't going to have to get poked with needles or spend time in the hospital. Along with everything I was taking to camp, I was also taking my crutches and my wheelchair. I would use the crutches for short distances and the wheelchair for longer distances.

Another great thing about the camp was that it wasn't only for sick kids. Their brothers and sisters could also go, so my little brother agreed to come with me. It was nice to have him along with me. It would give him a chance to have fun for a week, too. I was still very self-conscious about my appearance, so I made sure I had a baseball cap on my head at all times and that my leg was well hidden. I didn't want to get stared at by the other kids. But with camp being a place for other sick kids, I didn't get too many.

We loaded up on the buses and headed off to camp. The camp was about an hour away in Meridian, Texas, to the south of Dallas. I was quiet the entire ride to camp. I had this bad feeling that I wasn't going to like it. When we arrived at the camp there were a ton of people standing nearby on a porch with all kinds of signs. Most of these signs were to welcome us to the camp. As we exited the bus, you could hear loud music blaring as if it was some kind of party. As I carefully got off the bus, I had several people come up and welcome me to the camp. I was amazed at how friendly everyone was; it was as though these people had been my friends for years. We found our cabin counselors and fellow campers for the week and got settled in our cabin. The camp itself was beautiful. Off to one side was a lake with a fishing dock; on the other side was a huge red barn with a basketball court, and cabins dotted the camp. I had to admit: this was a great atmosphere. Way better than the hospital.

That first night, we had a candlelight ceremony to light a candle in remembrance of all the kids who had passed away. It made me so sad. The whole time since I'd been diagnosed death had been on my mind, and now I was going to have to look at pictures of kids who had passed away from cancer. It hit a little too close to home.

The candlelight ceremony was held at an outdoor chapel. Everyone from camp was there, and the ceremony began with a welcome and some singing. Then they brought out six candles for the ceremony. We were all given a little flashlight. As each kid's name was called out, we were to point our flashlight into the sky. The whole time we were doing this, I was overcome with fear. I began thinking, *Will my candle be lit next year?* At the same time, I knew we were remembering the lives led by these kids and that it wasn't all about death.

Because I was fifteen at the time, I was in the older boys' cabin. The age range of the campers was from six to sixteen. Since I was older, I got to choose my activities each day. I could choose from anything from sports and games to arts and crafts. I wasn't sure how much I would be able to participate because of my leg, but I went ahead and picked my activities anyway and thought I would at least give them a shot. I was getting more comfortable with the idea of being at camp. The counselors helped me to feel comfortable and helped me to have fun. I never felt like I was being looked at or judged. In a way, they treated me as if I'd never had cancer.

I started to see myself not as some cancer kid but as someone who was back in the real world. I was missing a leg but it
didn't seem to matter. I would hop from my bed to the bathroom and no one would look twice. It was the first time in a
long time I'd felt like a normal kid.

The other big thing that helped bring on this change in
my attitude was the other kids at camp. There were even a few
who'd had the same cancer as me, so we would share war stories. It was nice to talk to someone who knew what I was going through. We could relate to one another and it gave us a
chance to let it all out. There I was thinking I was the only one
in the world that was going through hell, losing friends in the
process, and feeling like it would never end; being able to see
that there were other kids going through the same thing felt
incredible to me.

Unfortunately, there were a few things I just couldn't do
and one of those things was swimming. Another thing was
water wars. Water wars was on held on Wednesday night in
the huge field next to the barn. Everyone would get out there
and play in the mud, just having a blast. It was fun to watch,
and I wished I could get out there and get all muddy. Later
that night, they had a firework show on the other side of the
lake. Being midway through camp, I felt like a new person and
was dreading the fact that camp would soon be over and that
I would have to return to reality. I didn't want to leave this
place—it was heaven.

The cherry on top was that a few of the guys in my cabin
had told me that one of the female campers thought I was cute.
"You guys must have the wrong guy," I told them.

"No way, man, she pointed you out to us and has been saying all week that she thinks you're cute." I was shocked.

"Who is she?" I asked. "Is she blind?" They pointed her
out to me.

"She's the one in the blue shorts," they said. I looked over and spotted the girl. At the time, it seemed like either a cruel joke or some kind of mix up, because this girl was gorgeous.

"You guys are lying," I told them. "No way a girl like that thinks I'm cute."

One of the guys shook his head at me. "Fine," he said. "I'll go ask her." He ran off before I could stop him. My face was red with embarrassment. He walked back and said "I told you, man, she totally thinks you're cute. You should go talk to her." All I could do was shake my head; I was way too overcome with shyness.

I couldn't believe a girl would actually think I was cute. I was skinnier than a toothpick, bald, and missing one leg. There was no way I was going to talk to this girl.

A little later that night, we were all making chicken fajitas over the fire. Being the shy kid, I was kind of off to the side. I looked over and noticed the girl the guys had been telling me about. A few minutes later, she started to make her way over to me. *Ah, crap,* I thought. *What do I do?*

"Hi," she said. "I'm Marisa." I was shocked and surprised that she'd actually walked up and started talking to me.

"Hi, I'm Scott," I mumbled. She told me that her sister had had cancer and that's why she was at the camp. She'd been coming for a few years now and really liked it—also, it was a great way to meet new people. The whole time she was talking to me, I felt like this was too good to be true. This girl was gorgeous and had chosen to come talk to me out of all the other people at the camp! She mentioned that her sister had also had an amputation. She had a sibling that had gone through what I was going through, so none of this was new to her. After being told that, I began to feel more comfortable and started to open up to her. The remainder of camp, we tried to see each other as much as we could. I even got to meet her sister. Her sister was younger and every bit as sweet as Marisa. Her name was Monica, and she could tell that I liked her sister, so she couldn't resist giving me a hard time and joking around with me.

As the last day of camp grew near, I became very sad. I never would've thought I could have enjoyed the camp as much as I had—especially considering my attitude when I'd first heard about it. I felt like a new person. I was happier, and my self-esteem was beginning to rise. I was feeling more confident in myself and very blessed. I had made some really great new friends and I wasn't sure if I was ever going to see them again. I was especially sad that I had actually managed to meet a girl I might never see again. We exchanged phone numbers and promised to keep in touch.

It was great for me, and for kids like me, to be in that kind of an environment—one where we didn't have to feel like sick kids. In my hometown, I was known as "that cancer kid who lost his leg," but at camp I was just "Scott." Better yet, I got to meet a ton of kids who had beaten cancer and they gave me hope that I was going to beat it myself. I got to share stories and say the kind of things that I couldn't say to anyone else. They understood me and they knew what I was going through at the time. Most of all, I got to be worry-free for a week. That week I felt like myself again and it was nice knowing that I wasn't alone.

12

THE OPENING PITCH

The one thing I was excited to go back home for was to see my parents and my brother. I was also excited because I was going to throw out the first pitch at a Texas Rangers game. This was around my fifteenth birthday and my aunt had written the Rangers management team a letter. She wanted to give me a birthday gift and she thought, what better gift than to be able to throw out the first pitch at a Rangers game? Once they read the letter, they informed my aunt that I would be granted the opportunity. The day we headed home from camp, I was to head out to the ballpark later that afternoon.

My parents were eager to hear about my week at camp. My mom was worried the whole week that I wouldn't like it because I had not wanted to go in the first place. They were glad to hear that I'd had a blast and to see a change in my attitude.

I'm a huge baseball fan and it was one of my goals to get back to playing. It was even more exciting knowing that the Rangers were playing the Seattle Mariners. I was a huge fan of Ken Griffey, Jr.

We got to the ballpark a few hours before the game on account of me having to check in and be instructed on what I was going to do when the time came for me to throw my pitch. After that, we went to our seats located on the third baseline a few rows up from the foul ball pole.

We were there early and there weren't too many other people there yet to watch batting practice. Out of all the games I've been to, I brought my glove for the first time since we were sitting so close to the foul line. It wasn't like I was going to run and try to catch a ball, but for some reason I decided to bring it with me that day. A few batters got through batting practice and, finally, the man I'd been waiting to see approached the plate. I was in awe watching him practice.

I had admired Ken Griffey, Jr. for as long as I could re-member and now I was actually in the same ballpark as him, watching him play. You could hear the crack of the bat and every now and then watch the ball fly over the wall. Then, all of a sudden, it happened. He hit a high fly ball that looked like it might make it to my section. The ball was coming closer and closer. I found myself thinking if I stood up I just might be able to catch it—it was that close. But I stayed seated, thinking that wind or something else would stop it from coming to me. Staring in amazement at the ball coming toward me in what seamed like slow motion, something told me to put my glove up in the air. As I did, the ball fell right into my glove. I made the catch! I brought my glove down and looked inside and saw the ball that Ken Griffey, Jr. had just hit. Then I heard applause from everybody around me and in sections next to mine. I couldn't believe it! This was turning out to be the best day of my life. I admired the ball. I didn't think my smile would ever leave my face.

As it got close to game time, we made our way back down to the field. I took the ball with me, hoping I might get the chance to see Ken Griffey, Jr. up close and possibly get it auto-graphed. As I crutched myself onto the field, I was so happy to be there. My mom, my aunt, my friend Frankie, and I were all standing in front of the Texas Rangers dugout. I was so excited to see all the players. That was when we noticed a guy dressed in regular clothes sitting in the dugout and chatting with the players. My mom asked one of the employees if it was OK for me to go sit in the dugout and meet some of the players. We were quickly told that was not possible because they didn't want the players to have any distractions right before a game. This didn't go over too well with my mother.

"He can't even sit in the dugout?" she asked. "It's hard for him to just stand there on his crutches because he's missing a leg."

"Sorry, he should be going out to throw the pitch here in a few minutes," said the employee. I couldn't believe they wouldn't let me meet any of the players—that they wouldn't even let me sit in the dugout.

"Well, he caught a ball that Ken Griffey, Jr. hit; can he at least just meet him since that's his favorite player? Could he have someone take the ball over to him to get it signed?" asked my mom.

"Sorry we can't do that," he said.

The guy looked at me and could tell that I was disappoint-ed. "Brett Hull is going to throw out the pitch with you. He just got signed by the Dallas Stars. Would you like to meet him?" he asked.

"No thanks," I said.

"Not a hockey fan?" he asked. "This guy is a well-known hockey player."

"No," I told him. "I'm not really a hockey fan." I was start-ing to feel that I wasn't being treated equally when I realized this Brett Hull guy was the one in the dugout.

As we were getting ready to head out onto the field, Brett Hull came up to me and introduced himself. What with me not knowing who he was, I didn't have much to say to the guy. By his expression, he seemed a little surprised that I wasn't a fan. As we walked onto the field near the pitcher's mound, my friend Frankie was walking with me so he could hold my crutches when I threw out the pitch.

Frankie and I walked up onto the mound and looked at each other with big grins on our faces. We took in the fact that we were on a pitcher's mound in a professional baseball park. *Amazing!* "You got it, man. Throw that strike," Frankie cheered. I looked over at my mom and aunt, their cameras flashing like crazy. I looked down at the catcher. As I gave Frankie my crutches, I made sure I had good balance on my one leg before I let go. I looked down at the ball for a moment and admired it. I looked up once more at the catcher and, standing on my one leg, swung my arm around and let the ball release from my hand.

It was pretty much a perfect strike, and man-oh-man, did it feel good to finally throw it. There was loud applause from the crowd as the catch was made. As I was crutching back to my mom and aunt, a few of the players came out from the dugout. They were all saying things like "Good job, kid" and "That was a nice throw." Once again, that smile came back to my face. Even while crutching close to the wall to exit the field, there were people in the stands congratulating me. Even though I didn't get to meet Ken Griffey, Jr., it was a moment I will always keep with me.

After that weekend I was due back in the hospital for another round of treatment. It was about mid-July and it was getting close to the end of my protocol of chemotherapy. It was exciting to know that I was coming to the end of treatment; that I was beginning to see the light at the end of the tunnel. Even though my attitude was better and my hope was stronger than before, I was still sick from the chemo and wishing I didn't have to keep having the treatments. It made my stays at the hospital easier when I got to talk to Marisa from camp and see her whenever I could.

It seemed like all my worries had lessened, because she was all I could think about. We would talk off and on multiple times a week. I even went out to the movies with her on one occasion. That was a huge step for me because I was afraid of being out in public. But knowing I was going to be with her, those fears didn't seem so big. I was really beginning to fall for her. But just as quickly as we met, our romance would eventually die off. As a month or so went by, we didn't talk as much. I heard less from her and when I did get the chance to talk to her she always seemed busy and less interested in me. This was pretty hard. Before camp, I had thought that a girl would never find me attractive; when I met her, she proved me wrong. But in just a short time, we were losing touch and I couldn't help but think it was because of me. Because my self-esteem was so low, I figured she'd come to see what I truly looked like, and that with her being back at school, she forgot about me. I was back to thinking, *What girl wants to date a guy with one leg?*

13

BACK TO LIVING

I was on my last month of chemotherapy treatment. September 16th, 1998, was my last round. For my last day in the hospital, my mom threw a small pizza party for me in my hospital room. She and a few members of the staff had decorated my door, and some nurses and friends came by to sign the poster on my door. *I did it!* I was finally finishing up my last round of chemo and I wouldn't have to come back for more treatments. It was a very exciting day for me and for my family. I had come so far. Eight or nine months before I faced a serious disease and I was very afraid of what was going to happen to me. Death seemed to be just around the corner. I had week after week of treatments; I got sick time after time. It was one of the hardest things I have ever had to do in my life and

I was still standing—only now on just one leg. Not only was I broken down physically and emotionally but my life had changed socially, too.

For most of those months of treatment I had been sad and alone. I lived my life in fear of what the days ahead held for me. Even on my last day of treatment, I knew I was about to face another test. It was far from over. As I exited the door of my hospital room and was showered with silly string, applause, and congratulations, it was good to know that I was beating cancer and that I'd made a promise to myself to continue to fight. I wasn't going to let it get me. I was ready to go on with my life.

But, of course, saying things is always easier than doing things. It seemed like the day after my last treatment I was in a constant state of worry. Even though I didn't have any more chemo treatments ahead of me, I was afraid of the cancer coming back. I had heard too many stories from other kids about how they would finish up their rounds of chemo, be OK for a few months, and then the cancer would suddenly return. Knowing this, I had myself convinced it was going to happen to me. Even though I had completed my protocol, I had to return to the hospital each month for six months for checkups. I would still have my blood drawn to check my blood counts. I would still have to have chest X-rays, MRIs, CAT scans, and bone scans. These checkups were all-day events.

Another thing I had to do was breathing treatments. The breathing treatments were to keep my lungs clear while recovering from the chemotherapy and the drugs my body I was being weaned off.

Now you'd think I'd be happy to get back to a normal life but to be honest, I *wanted* to be at the hospital. I felt safer at the hospital. If I had a pain, I wanted a scan done right then and there. I didn't care if the pain was at the tip of my finger; I wanted to have a test run. I was so scared that the cancer was going to come back. I would be at home watching television and all of a sudden get indigestion and I'd burst into tears, convinced that the cancer was back. Every time I had a checkup, Dr. Murray had to convince me that I was clear of cancer and that things were looking good. After living my life in fear for so long, it all seemed too good to be true: I just couldn't believe I was really free of it.

How do you change your way of thinking when all you've been doing is preparing yourself for the worst? That was how I lived most of my days. I prepared for the worst and hoped for the best. I mean, one day I was told I was fine; a month later, I was told that I had cancer. It was kind of hard not to worry.

One good thing was that I was off chemo, which meant I could start getting fitted for my prosthesis. Not only was I happy to be getting my leg, but it got my mind off of the fear that I was living in with the thought of the cancer returning. Instead of going back to Nova Care, we thought it best to go to Scottish Rite Children's Hospital in Dallas, Texas, to get fitted for my prosthesis. The funding for the leg was being completely taken care of, which gave my parents some relief from all the other medical bills pilling up. I had appointments a few times a week and underwent the same process I had gone through with Nova Care. This time it seemed to take longer because I really didn't have much else going on and I was so ready to get my leg. Each time I would go for a fitting, the test fitting would be unsuccessful— because the fitting was either too loose or too tight. And, when it comes to the fitting of a prosthesis, the fit has to be just right.

It was during the month of December that all this was happening and I was hoping and praying that I would have my leg by Christmas. I wanted to be around my family and friends with two legs instead of one. I had my heart set on it. Thanks to my lack of knowledge about all that went in to the fitting of a prosthesis, I was disappointed and I didn't get my leg by Christmas. I was once again coming to the realization that all of this was going to be very, very hard. Just as I had overcome the obstacle of cancer, I was now taking on the new challenge of being an amputee.

I was still without a prosthesis when it came time for my last surgery. This surgery was to take the port out of my chest where I had received my chemo treatments. This would be my fifth surgery in less than a year but I was ready to have that port out of my body. The surgery went well and after staying in the hospital for a few days I was back home. Christmas came and I got to spend another holiday with my family. This time of the year was very emotional for me, even though I tried to hide it. While spending time with my family, I would also be thinking, *What if this is the last holiday I ever get to spend with them?* Never would I have thought this before I got sick, but having gone through what I went through and having been so close to death, I had these feelings often . . . and I still do to this day. I would hide away by myself, when my emotions would overtake me, and cry. I'd cry because I was thankful that I was still here, and I would cry because I was still so scared of dying.

A few weeks after Christmas I was back at Scottish Rite to get my leg. Since I couldn't just put my leg on and walk out of the hospital, I had to undergo physical therapy to learn how to walk again. With us being an hour and a half away from the hospital, and with them telling me I needed to undergo physical therapy twice a day for a couple of weeks, my parents thought it was best for me to stay at the hospital. My mom was going to stay with me for those two weeks while my dad went to work and my brother went to school. The stay at the hospital wasn't too bad because the rooms weren't like regular hospital rooms; they were like rooms straight out of a nice hotel.

I had to do leg exercises on my own when I wasn't in the therapy gym. Alone in my room, I would exercise my leg to build up the muscles. While in the therapy gym, I was getting a taste of the realities of learning to walk again. It was tough. I was placed between a set of parallel bars so I could hold on to them while I had my new leg on. While standing on the new leg, I was asked how it felt. I wasn't sure how to answer because it was all so new to me. I didn't know what the prosthesis was supposed to feel like so I had a hard time trying to explain it. While standing on the leg, the prosthetic people were trying to make sure that the knee and the foot lined up with my body and were on point. This was a big part of the fitting process. The first day of therapy I didn't even take any steps because they had to get all the adjustments done first. This was a very frustrating and prolonged process. I was overwhelmed by what had to be done before even taking my first step.

Finally the day came and I was able to take a few steps. Even though I was ready in my mind, my body was not ready. My balance was completely off. I was pretty much like a toddler learning how to walk. I had a tight grip on the bars and was afraid if I let go I was going to face plant on the floor. Down at the other end of the parallel bars was a tall mirror. Every now and then I would look up at the mirror to see what I looked like. I was disgusted and embarrassed by what I saw reflected back at me. All the while, I was trying to accept this was the new me. Learning to walk on my prosthesis was an experience in itself. I wanted to just take the leg and throw it across the room because it just didn't feel like it was a part of me. I felt unattractive, I had trouble getting the leg on and walking seemed impossible. It all combined in such a way that moved me right over the edge of frustration.

A few days went by and I was no better at walking. My confidence, already at an all-time low, was now shattered. It all seemed impossible. I was quick-

ly losing hope that I would ever walk on my own—
let alone play sports. I did what I was told in therapy
and trusted them when they told me that I would
one day not only walk, but I would play sports again.

So I worked hard. By the second week, I was taking a few small steps with just one hand on the bars.
It didn't seem like much to me at the time, but it was
a big accomplishment and a major step toward my
recovery.

I slowly improved; with just one hand on the bars
it was pretty much like using a cane. I moved to the
next logical step: walking with a cane. This was very
scary for me. I was afraid that I was going to fall and
hurt myself. I had to wear a safety belt around my
waist as I slowly took step after step. It wasn't perfect,
but I was walking. Those first few steps wiped me out.
My energy was gone and my endurance, like everything else, was just one more thing I needed to work
on in therapy.

It was coming up on the last days of my stay at
Scottish Rite and I was only putting on my leg for a
couple of hours at a time each day. Being a new amputee and having my first prosthesis, I was going to
have to work up to wearing my leg throughout the
day. I started with just two hours a day and slowly
worked up to three or four hours a day. I continued
through this process even after I left Scottish Rite.

I did not like the feeling of the prosthesis. It felt
like I had a huge chunk of metal attached to my limb.
It was so uncomfortable it made it almost impossible
for me to imagine any kind of future mobility.

Despite all of this frustration, I never once regretted my decision to have the amputation. I knew it was all about the cards you'd been dealt and the cards you need to play the game. One of those cards was getting used to my temporary leg—the first one was the one I learned to walk on, a kind of beginner leg, and a better one would come when I was ready for it. By the time I left the Scottish Rite, I was using a cane and walking very slowly and carefully.

The day-to-day realities of having a prosthesis were proving to be interesting. Upon waking, the first thing I had to do before anything else was to put my leg on. It was going to be a routine thing, just like brushing my teeth. When I went to sleep at night, I would take it off. As for taking a shower or a bath, I could do whichever I wanted. When showering I would balance on one leg—something I was getting really good at!

But other things weren't as easy to get used to, especially the noise my socket would occasionally make if it lost air or became loose. All of this occurred because I had what you called a "suction socket." There was a hole cut out towards the end of my socket and I was to slide the skin of my stump down into the socket. Once my stump was all the way in, I was to take a valve piece and screw it on, creating a suction to help hold the socket in place. To take my leg off, I would unscrew the valve, or press the button on the valve, and release the air in my socket. The system wasn't perfect and sometimes, while walking, my skin would move in such a way that would cause slight gaps or air pockets to form. Air pockets, or air bubbles, would then pop as I was walking, making a very distinctive sound . . . that being the sound of someone letting one rip. *Brutal, right?* Needless to say, I hated it when that happened and it only made me more self-conscious.

Add to that the fact that my balance was still way off. I had to stay still when someone passed me because if they happened to brush by me too closely, I would feel like I was going to fall. I stayed close to things and away from people. While at home, I practiced as much as I could. As for going out in public, I still wasn't comfortable. I was embarrassed about the way I looked. This is something that has stayed with me. I was extremely nervous about returning to school. I hadn't talked to or seen anyone from school in months and I knew I was going to get a lot of stares. My hair was slowly growing back but it was coming in black—much darker than it had been before I got cancer.

14

GETTING IN THE GAME

The day finally came. Since I was only wearing my leg for about three or four hours at a time, I returned to school for the afternoon classes only. The plan was to take about two or three classes at a time to slowly get back into the swing of things. I was terrified about returning to a social environment. How were the people who knew me going to react? I had a ton of questions and fears running through my mind as my mom drove me to school. When we pulled up, I saw kids walking into the school. I just sat there because I didn't want to get out of the car. I didn't want to return to school. I wasn't comfortable with who I was, and I was scared of the reactions I was going to get.

"You're going to be OK, Scott," my mom told me. "I know you're scared, but you can do this. Just think about all you have been through already. This is nothing."

I nodded my head in agreement and slowly exited the car. As I took slow steps into the school with my cane, my nerves were going crazy. I wore pants because I didn't want to draw any more attention to myself than I was already going to get. As I walked down the hall to my class, I was concentrating hard on keeping my balance and praying to God that no one would bump me by accident. I recognized some people so I made eye contact with them, but they quickly looked the other way. I was confused. I knew these people knew who I was, so why were they just walking past me? I felt like the new kid at school all over again. Like nobody knew who I was. As I got to my class, I quickly took my seat. As more people arrived, I kept getting the same reaction. No one knew what to do, and no one approached me. I wasn't expecting people to come up to me and talk my ear off, but I wasn't thinking that they would just ignore me either. It really hurt me inside, and I couldn't wait for the school day to be over.

Pretty soon I started to hear whispering like, "That's that kid that had cancer," and "That's Scott. He had cancer." So now I knew they knew who I was, but still, no one approached me. That's pretty much how the first day of school went—not fun. I didn't talk to anybody, and nobody talked to me. I just heard my name whispered as I walked down the halls, as if I had some contagious disease. Nobody talked to me, but everybody was talking *about* me. This made me even more insecure.

The whole semester was horrible. I couldn't wait to get out of school, and I felt like I had no friends. The people I had played ball with and the people who knew me before all of a sudden didn't seem to know me anymore. Not one girl looked my way, and when a girl did look at me, I got this disgusted look like I was some kind of a freak. It was all proving my theory right: why would a girl be interested in a guy with one leg? I was becoming angry. *How dare these people treat me like they don't know me? Who are these people to think they are better than me?* And soon I began to get this drive to prove them wrong.

When the semester was finally over, I was determined to work my butt off—not only to get to my goal of getting back to sports, but also to show these people that I was the same person and that I could play ball again. That summer, I was finally at the point where I was wearing my leg for the majority of the day. My energy was still low and I was still weak in areas, but I wanted to return to basketball and baseball when school started back up in August. This meant that I only had almost four months to get ready. I knew it was going to be hard to do on my own, so I made the decision to get back into physical therapy to build my strength and endurance.

My mom began to call around to local outpatient therapy places to see if they would be able to work with me. She would begin to tell them my story, and they would all tell her the same thing: I was going to have to face the reality that there were going to be certain things that I would never be able to do again. They said all they could really teach me was how to get through my daily activities—something I was already doing. With that, my mom made her last call of the day to Huguley Outpatient Therapy. She went through the whole routine with them as she did with the other calls . . . only this time, the response was, "That's awesome! We can't wait to meet him!" We knew then that we'd found the right place for us.

Huguley was only about a fifteen-minute drive from our house, and the plan was to do physical therapy three times a week. It entailed a lot more strength training exercises and more work on my balance. Around this time, I was walking on my own and no longer needed a cane.

I worked my butt off that whole summer. There were days when I didn't want to go because I knew it was going to be tough, but if I ever wanted to get back on the field I knew that this was something I had to do. The staff was behind me all the way and believed in me, which helped with my recovery. With their attitude rubbing off on me, I was slowly becoming more confident. I also knew that the only person who could stop me was me.

It was during my first month at Huguley that I was first approached to go to a running clinic for amputees. The clinic was taught by two amputees that competed in the Paralympic Games. My parents and I woke up early one Saturday morning to attend the clinic. I was really excited to see an amputee run.

When we arrived at the YMCA in Dallas, I was approached by one of the amputees who taught the clinic.

"Who is this guy we got here?" he asked me with a big smile. "Man, you look like an athlete." I thought, *This guy must be crazy.* "Well, Scott, I hope you're ready because we are going to get you running today," he told me. I just smiled, told him my name, and then shook my head as if he was full of it. *How was I going to learn to run in one day when it had taken me forever to learn how to walk again?*

The first step was to teach us the proper kinds of stretches and exercises that would help an amputee with running. This was all part of the first session and occurred before we broke for lunch. The second part of the clinic was going to be a demonstration. Like I said, I was eager to see an amputee run. It seemed impossible to me, and I wanted to see how it was done. As the second part of the day got underway, the first thing they did was to ask for a volunteer. Nobody raised their hand, so the guy I'd met earlier yelled out, "Hey, there's the guy that I said was going run today!" Oh, no! I was the volunteer.

He asked me to come up to the front and took me through the different types of exercises, or steps, that were all a part of learning how to run with a prosthesis. I began by placing my prosthesis in front of me with my good leg behind me. Then I learned how to transfer my good leg behind me while putting my weight *through* my prosthesis. After doing this for a couple of minutes, I was asked to take another step—

only now I *kicked* my prosthesis through as fast as I could and stopped when my heel stuck the ground. I went from one hop-step to two hop-steps and then to three hop-steps. It felt really weird. I had both the trainers on either side of me because I was scared I was going to fall.

After that, I did another exercise where I would take baby steps and kick my prosthesis forward as fast as I could—then kick back just as fast. This was teaching me to kick both the front and back walls of my socket in an effort to control it and get my leg moving at a new speed.

After doing all these different types of exercises, they took me to the track. I was going to put it all together and try to run. I told the trainers they better be right beside me and hold onto my hands.

"You can do this, man," they told me. "Just concentrate and use the steps we taught you. You got this!" After taking a moment, I did some tentative hop-jump steps. One hop-jump turned into two, then two into three, and before I knew it I had taken ten steps. It wasn't the prettiest thing to behold, but I was running. I couldn't believe it! Even though it wasn't perfect—or normal-looking—it was another hurdle that I'd overcome and something I never thought I would do again.

I now had another set of tools to help me get back to my old athletic self. The following week I showed my therapist what I'd learned, and running became another part of my program. I was starting to see the kinds of changes I'd been waiting for—it was finally coming together. I was getting stronger and more used to my prosthesis.

I had to go to another place to get my prosthetic care: Nova Care. This was the place I had originally gone to, but it was now called Hanger Prosthetics. I was to have a new person taking care of me, and I hoped it would be someone who believed in me and my goals. When I went back for my first checkup, I was greeted by an upbeat lady with a huge smile on her face. When I first met Phyllis and we talked about what I wanted to do, I knew she was the person for me. She had more faith in me than I did. She was excited and couldn't wait for me to get back on the field.

The changes weren't only physical but mental, too. It did so much for my confidence to realize that some of the stuff I had thought was impossible was now possible. I continued therapy for about two more months. A byproduct of having my leg on for longer and longer periods of time was that I was picking up things and learning how things should feel. If something didn't feel right, I went back to Hanger to get it adjusted or fixed. I was doing all kinds of exercises too.

I would usually be at therapy for a good hour. First I did a warmup on the bike, then over to the mat to do some leg exercises like kicking my leg in all different directions to build up the muscles in my stump. I would then work on some balance exercises by stepping on a mini trampoline and trying to stand on it with just my prosthesis. They would also put a strap with weights attached around my waist, and I would walk forwards, backwards, and sideways to work on my balance. These exercises were now a part of my life and would be something I would always have to go through as an amputee.

Toward the last month of therapy, I was out on the basketball court shooting hoops and trying to get used to bouncing a ball while moving around with my leg on. While I was at home I would do this—even when I didn't have my leg on, I would hop around the court and just shoot. I would even play a game or two with my brother and a few friends without my leg. I had pretty good balance. But while I was in therapy, I was practicing with my leg on and trying to get used to it. It was tough, but it was just another one of those things that had seemed impossible.

I was wearing my leg more, but it wasn't always the most comfortable thing to wear. I had days when my leg was sore and felt heavier than it did on other days. It would also rub me at the top of my socket and leave my skin red and tender. As I became more mobile and tried new things, I would have times (since my socket was so high on my hip) that it would catch and pinch my business. Needless to say, that was painful. As time went on, I was able to tell when I couldn't put all my weight on my leg because I'd pinch myself.

One big thing I had to be careful of was that my stump was all the way down in my socket. If I was not all the way down, there would be problems. If I wasn't careful, I could cut the circulation off at the bottom of my stump and get what is known as a pressure sore. I needed constant contact at the bottom of my socket to keep the circulation going and avoid a sore, but since I was a new amputee it was hard to tell and over time I did develop one. It was painful, and the only way for it to heal was to stay off my leg and wear what's called a "shrinker." A shrinker looks like panty hose and helps with circulation and the proper forming of the stump. After having a pressure sore and going through that experience, I learned what to look for and what my prosthesis should feel like.

A prosthetic limb has a big learning curve that can be very frustrating at times. Every time I pulled my leg on, I had to be sure I was all the way down in my socket and that my leg was on good and straight. If not, it meant the chance of developing a pressure sore—or worse, some pinched business!

My balance was better but not all there yet. Once done with therapy, I did as much as I could on my own. I was constantly on my leg when I could tolerate it.

I was getting excited around that time because camp was coming up. This year, I couldn't wait to go. I was sixteen, so this was going to be my last year as a camper. While I was happy to go, I was sad that I might not be able to return.

The second year at camp was just as good as the first. This time I had my leg and was off treatment. I found myself chatting with other kids and giving them hope because I was now someone that had finished treatment and was doing well, whereas last year I was the sick one who was having a tough time. Although I was a camper, it felt good to share my story and to see that I was helping kids have hope. By the end of camp, I knew in my heart that I wanted to return as a counselor. As long as I was still alive and Camp Sanguinity existed, I made a pact with myself to return each year in hopes of giving back to the camp that had helped me so much.

I returned home from camp in time for my sixteenth birthday. Like every other kid who reaches this milestone, I wanted a car. I was blessed and thankful that I got my wish: an old Chevy truck. This meant learning how to drive with no right leg. *How was this going to work?*

I brought this problem up with Phyllis, and she said I had two options. I could either have hand controls to drive, or I could learn to drive with my left foot. She said she could install what was called a "knee crosser" right above my knee, so that when I pushed a button I could bend my prosthesis to the side and move it out of the way. With the knee crosser, I learned how to drive with my left foot. It really wasn't that hard. The knee crosser also helped me put pants and shoes on—way easier than doing it with a straight leg.

By late August, I was back at school. Every day at school I wore pants because I was still so self-conscious. No one talked to me, and I talked to no one. Instead of feeling sad and upset, I tried my best to put it aside and concentrate on my goals. I'm not going to lie and say I didn't have my days where I'd go home and cry because I felt like nobody liked me or that I was being judged because of what had happened to me. But like I said, I turned it into motivation.

Since I now had a vehicle, I needed to learn some responsibility and find a job. So I went down to the small local grocery store and applied for one. The job didn't seem too difficult, and it was close to my house. A few weeks later, I got a call saying that I had gotten the job. With this being my first job, I was a little nervous. With a new leg, I was even more nervous. I was going to be a sacker for the store, so that meant tons of walking and carrying bags throughout the day.

Doing my best, I worked through the pain I would sometimes have in my leg. I wanted to be like everyone else that worked there. I didn't want to be the "handicapped" or "disabled" kid that worked at the store. This job was the first time that I actually got to talk to and really be friends with kids my own age. At school I was ignored and looked at differently. But with work, I was forced to communicate with others to get the job done. I wanted friends, and it was nice to know I had friends at work. Looking back, I may have been in want of friends a little too much.

Football season was starting, and the basketball off-season was beginning as well. Basketball was a sport I loved and wanted to get back to, so I signed up for the off-season as a way to be ready for the season. I remember walking into the classroom where the first team meeting was being held. It felt like all the guys looked at me as if I didn't deserve to be there, as if I was only allowed in there because it was the charitable thing to do. I sat quietly by myself while the others interacted with each other as if I wasn't there. When it came time to head to the gym, I waited until all the other kids left the room so I could talk to the coach alone.

"Coach," I said, "My name is Scott Odom, and—I don't know if you know this or not—I am an amputee. I don't want you to treat me any differently just because I have one leg."

"I know who you are," he said. "I won't treat you differently. If there's something you know you can't do or don't feel comfortable doing, just let me know, and we will work around it." After our talk, I made my way to the locker room. I sat on the end of a bench with my locker in front of me and my bag beside me. I stared at the locker. I was nervous to change in front of everybody because of my leg, and I wasn't comfortable with the stares I knew I would get.

I sat quietly until all the guys left the locker room. When the last guy had finally left, I changed my clothes. I knew they knew I only had one leg, but this was going to be the first time they were going to see my prosthesis. I was nervous about what I was going to have to do as far as drills because I wasn't completely secure with my prosthesis and wasn't yet able to do all the things I wanted to do. Still sitting there, I heard the door open. It was the coach.

"You about ready there, Scott?" he asked me.

"I think so," I told him. "Just taking a moment here before I go out. I am a little nervous."

He said, "You know you've got to go out there if you want to play. If you want, you can just stand off to the side and watch for today if that will make you more comfortable."

Finally getting the courage to make my way to the gym, I followed the coach out onto the floor. I took a look at the group of guys huddled up, and everyone's eyes were on my leg. I quickly found a spot to the side of the court where I could hide my leg behind a table and watch practice. I was embarrassed, and I wanted practice to be over as soon as possible. How was I going to overcome this? How was I going to play a game I loved if I couldn't find the courage to show my leg?

The next day I found myself to the side once again, watching practice. It killed me to watch a sport I loved to play. I guess Coach could tell I was working up the courage to make a move because before I knew it I heard him say, "Odom, you want to get in on this drill?" Without a word, I slowly made my way to the floor and got in a line for the shooting drill.

I love to shoot a basketball, so I figured this was a drill that would help me calm my nerves. While going through the drill, I tried to block out the stares and the whispers. As I began to knock down a couple of shots, the drive and motivation that had been there but blocked by my low self-esteem took over. Even though I was self-conscious, I was doing something that I loved to do, and I suddenly didn't care what other people were thinking of me.

I knew the only person that was going to stop me from playing was me, so I definitely wasn't going to let a bunch of guys keep me from my goals. Weeks went by, and I continued to tough it out during the drills and the workout routines. I may have needed a little more time or was last on some of the drills, but I made sure I finished. Even though I was active in the basketball off-season, I was still far off from where I needed to be to play at a high level. I still wasn't comfortable with my leg, and there were days when it hurt just to walk on it.

I found myself having to make a decision. Baseball was the other sport I really wanted to get back to as an amputee, and if I went back as pitcher, it would be less active than basketball. I decided it was better if I concentrated on baseball. I felt ready. I decided to get out of basketball and work on baseball.

This was one of the hardest decisions for me to make. One reason was that I loved basketball and hated the fact that I wouldn't be able to play, but most of all, I had never quit a sport in my life! I tried looking at it as though I was making a smart decision. As soon as I got out of basketball, I told Coach D that I was ready to start playing baseball again. It was nice to play under Coach D because he already knew me and would help me get to the point where I could compete again.

For the next two months, I played catch as much as I could and worked on my pitching. Even though I was still ignored and left by myself at school, there were a few athletes who helped me with my pitching or offered to be my throwing partner. Slowly, I was making new friends. Baseball season finally came around, and I was excited to finally get to play.

I started as pitcher on the second game of the season. I was so pumped. Even with the excitement of starting a game, I still had a part of me that doubted myself. I had never had this feeling before I'd gotten sick. I now knew that I wasn't the best baseball player on the field and I couldn't play like I used to. I was fighting with myself to get all the bad images out of my head. That game was the first time I was really scared to go out and play, even though this was what I had worked so hard for. I wanted to last more than a couple of innings and put the ball in play. That was my goal going into the game.

I knew I didn't have the best stuff as a pitcher, and I didn't throw the ball the hardest, but I just wanted to do my best. When I arrived at the ballpark, I sat in my truck and took a moment to mentally prepare myself. This was it. This was my chance to prove to everybody that I was back and that I could still play ball. I had to face it: being an amputee meant that I would get stares no matter how much I didn't want them. We were playing Stephenville at home, and word had it that they were a good team.

As I was warming up with the catcher, I was saying prayer after prayer to God to watch over me and give me the strength I needed to get through the game. I knew this was going to be a test for me.

Game time finally arrived, and the visiting team was first at bat. I took a step back from the pitcher's mound and took a moment to take it all in. I looked over at the bleachers and saw my family. I had my own cheering section. I let it all sink in that I was back in the game. I looked over to the visiting dugout and gave a slight smile. Not to be cocky but to let them know that I planned to play my heart out. The first batter came to the plate. My first pitch was a fastball—with a swing and a miss!

"Strike!" yelled the umpire. A loud cheer erupted; this was going to be fun. I kept telling myself over and over that I could do this—and it worked. A few pitches later, I recorded my first strikeout. As the ball was being thrown around the horn, my teammates told me what a good job I was doing. It felt amazing. I knew in my heart that this was going to be my game. The third inning came around, and I was still in the game. Not only was I still in the game, but I had recorded five strikeouts. I had given up a few hits but no runs so far. The cheering was getting louder and louder as the game went on. I could tell some of my teammates were shocked. Most of them had never seen anything like it. Heck, I was shocked myself.

I had to choose if I wanted to bat or have a designated hitter hit for me. I chose the designated hitter because I was confident in my batting but not my running.

As the game went on, it was getting better and better for me. My team was racking up the runs. By the fifth inning, the score was 8–1. My confidence was through the roof. I felt like there was nothing I couldn't do out there on the mound. My knuckleball was confusing the batters, and I had gotten nine strikeouts in the first five innings. I couldn't believe it! I was definitely in the zone.

By the sixth inning, my strikeout total was up to eleven. I was unstoppable. My next pitch was a fast-ball. The batter swung and made contact with the ball, and it was a hard line shot—right at *me*.

I didn't know it had hit me until I saw the ball on the ground in front of me. Luckily for me, the ball hit my prosthetic leg. I picked it up and threw the guy out at first. My coach and teammates ran up to me and asked if I was OK.

"Scott! Are you hurt?" they asked.

"I'm fine," I told them with a laugh. "The ball hit my prosthetic leg. I didn't feel a thing!" The others started to laugh too. The coach headed back to the dugout, and I got ready for the next batter. The very first pitch was a strike. The strike seemed to calm things down for me.

The next pitch was another hard line drive right at me. This time, it hit the tip of my glove, just missing my wrist. Now that one scared the crap out of me! In shock, I wasn't able to locate the ball in time to get the runner out at first base. As soon as the play was over, my coach and the players ran up to the mound again to see if I was OK. "I think they're aiming for you, Scott," my coach told me. "I'm going to take you out of the game before you get hurt."

I didn't want to come out of the game, but I wasn't the type of player to talk back to a coach. I didn't think the other team was intentionally aiming for me. That's just the way the game goes sometimes. Once he told me he wanted to take me out, I knew he was only doing it out of concern for my safety.

I was taken out of the game in the sixth inning with a new personal record. When I got to the bench and sat down, I still had a big grin on my face. It was a dream game. I'd pitched my heart out, and it had all fallen into place. I was so excited to see what more I could do as the season went on.

The next day at practice, Coach gave me the game ball from the night before, and it's a ball I will have with me forever.

The next big game was against my old school, Everman. This was going to be my second start, and I wasn't as nervous this time around. It was around this time that my parents wanted me to give batting a try. I had been a pretty good batter before I lost my leg, and they believed I still had it in me.

"Just hit it over the fence so that you don't have to run as fast around the bases," my dad said. "You can just take your time." I was still against the idea of batting because I felt I couldn't run very well.

In a neat twist of fate, Ken Griffey, Jr. had just been traded to the Cincinnati Reds. Being a big fan, I wanted his new jersey really bad. My parents made me a proposal: if I had just one at bat in a game, they would go out the next day and buy me the jersey. Man, what a hard deal to pass up!

I started thinking: if I struck out or walked, it would still be considered an at bat. So with the deal in hand, and knowing how much my parents wanted to see me in the batter's box again, I decided that during the game against Everman I would give it a shot.

I started out strong. I was toward the end of the line in the batting order, so I didn't get my chance at bat until the second inning. Already with a few strikeouts as a pitcher under my belt, my confidence was climbing. I grabbed a batting helmet and made my way to the on-deck circle.

There was only one out and no runners on base, meaning I was definitely going to bat this inning. Before I knew it, it was my turn at bat. When I put my foot in the batter's box all the old feelings came back—the good old feelings of wanting to drive the ball into the gap, making sweet contact with it. The pitcher wasn't throwing that hard, and I knew I could hit off of him.

I did my old routine in the box. I dug my cleats into the dirt and found a good comfortable spot to prepare for my swing. I looked at the pitcher dead on and swung the bat slowly, pointing at him, letting him know I was ready for whatever he threw at me. I already had it made in my mind not to take the first pitch. I wanted to see what I could expect from his pitches. The first pitch was a high ball. I stepped out and got a few more practice swings in before I returned to the box and got ready for the next pitch. I watched this one go by as well, only this time it was an inside strike. With the count one and one, I was feeling a little more comfortable. The next pitch came and I took a good cut and fouled it. I was now behind in the count, one and two, and had to swing at anything close. I was also thinking that my turn at bat was almost done—I could get that Griffey jersey tomorrow. Even though I wanted that jersey, I also wanted a base hit.

The next pitch was thrown and looked like it was coming down the middle. As I began my swing, the ball suddenly broke down as if falling off a table, and I swung and missed. He had gotten me on a good curve ball.

As I recovered from my swing, I heard everybody on my team start yelling "Run! *Run!*" I looked back at the catcher and realized he had missed the catch. A dropped pitch meant the batter had a chance to run and get safe on first before being thrown out. When I saw this, I thought, *You have got to be kidding me.*

My first at bat with my prosthesis was a dropped third strike. What were the odds? I dropped the bat and began my type of running. I was slowly making my way down to first base, wishing the ball would hurry up and get thrown so I could be out already and go back to the dugout. All eyes were on me, seeing me run for the very first time. It seemed like it took forever. As I got closer to the bag, the ball finally flew by me.

The throw was low, and the first baseman tried to scoop it up for the out but missed it. Thanks to another missed ball, I finally arrived at the bag safe and sound. My coach and parents were jumping up and down as if we'd just won the World Series. I stood there in disbelief. I'd done it! A pinch runner was sent to replace me, and I made my way to the dugout amidst deafening applause from the crowd. This was turning out to be another one of those games. A few more innings passed, and by the fifth inning I was due up again to bat.

The same pitcher was in the game, and I was determined this time to make contact with the ball. I wasn't going to go through that dropped-third–strike stuff again. The first pitch was thrown, and I sent it right back up the middle. A chest-high line drive up to center field, and I eventually made it to first base with a single to add to my day. When the game ended, I had served up nine strikeouts as a pitcher and had hit a single. Not only did I pitch a good game, I got to finish the game.

A few weeks later, the season came to an end. During that baseball season, I was back to my old self. I was doing the things that I loved to do and was having fun doing it. I didn't think about or worry about cancer. It was sports that had delivered a way for me to be happy and to be myself.

My senior year at Joshua High School came, and it meant I would play on the varsity team. I was extremely excited because I was finally going to play under Coach D again. Since I was to be on varsity, that letter jacket I had wanted since I was a little kid was to become a reality. I soon learned that Coach D was resigning as head baseball coach to join the police academy. I was upset to see him go because I loved to play for him, and I knew he knew what I could do on the field. The thought of getting a new coach scared me. *What if he didn't give me a chance?*

And that, unfortunately, was how my senior year on varsity played out. I had a bad feeling in the off season. The new coach really never paid any attention to me and during practices and drills would leave me out since I wasn't a starter and was just a relief pitcher. He would joke and talk to all the other players but seemed reluctant to do that with me.

I knew I was being judged because of my leg. When I came to this realization, it made me angry—especially because the season was underway, and we were without a win. Even halfway through the season, the new coach was still using the same two pitchers every other game. All I could do was ride the bench. I have never been so angry in my life. I could understand if we were winning games and had a good shot at the playoffs, but we hadn't won a single game. As the games went by, the innings felt longer and longer. I sat quietly on the bench like a ghost.

I also became angry with the other players' attitudes. They would joke around, being disrespectful and cocky. I would have given anything to have my leg back and play. I felt like they were taking baseball for granted, and that hurt.

Coming down to the last two games of the season, I had yet to set foot on the field. I decided one day after practice to confront the coach and tell him what was on my mind. I had kept too much bottled up and was at the point of losing it.

"Coach, can I talk to you before you leave?" I asked.

"Yeah, sure. What's on your mind?"

I took a deep breath and said, "We are down to the last two games of the season and we've not won a single game. I have yet to play, and I feel like you don't believe in me and that you don't think I can play. Please tell me right now if you plan on not playing me and I'll turn in my stuff. This is a waste of my time, and you have no idea how hard it is for me to sit on that bench and just watch."

"Oh, we're going to get you in a game, Scott," he told me. "I know we haven't won any games, and I was going to try to get you in a couple of times, but unfortunately it just didn't work out. You don't have to quit because, I promise, you will play in a game."

Given this talk (though not really feeling any better about the situation) I decided to wait it out and see what happened, to see if he stuck to his promise.

The last game of the season came and I was told a few hours before the game that I would be starting. As I was warming up, I felt upset and angry. I felt the only reason I was starting was because I had threatened to quit. No more words were exchanged between the coach and me. I was not comfortable with this start as pitcher because I knew it was for all the wrong reasons. The entire season I had been judged because of my leg and now, after I expressed my thoughts, I was starting the last game of the season. I saw it as sympathy, and I didn't like it.

The first batter came up and drove the ball to left center field. The next two batters did the same with base hits. I was not off to a good start. With three runs on the scoreboard, we finally got three outs.

Our bats went three up, three down, and I made my way back onto the mound. I walked the first batter, and the second batter hit a double to right field. The batter after that squared up to bunt and successfully pulled it off. A bunt was hard for me to get to because I wasn't as quick as everyone else. The batter after him also squared up to bunt and got safe on first. I thought two bunts in a row seemed kind of odd, but didn't think much about it. I was just trying to get an out. Then the next batter also squared up to bunt.

Three bunts in a row, and a loud roar of boos came from the crowd. It hit me what was happening. I was being taken advantage of. It wasn't enough to get base hits off of me, which is a normal part of the game, but to bunt three times in a row was playing dirty in my eyes.

Sure enough, the fourth batter squared up to bunt. After that batter, I looked over at their third base coach and just stared him down. He made slight eye contact but quickly looked down. What horrible sportsmanship. Angry and not in my right mind, I watched my coach make his way to the mound. My eyes began to water. I knew I was being taken out of the game and that this would be my last baseball game. When Coach finally arrived at the mound, before he could say a word to me, I handed him the ball and walked off the field with my head down.

As soon as I hit the bench, the tears started to roll. Sports were over for me. I had dreamed so long of becoming a professional athlete. I felt like my passion to play was being ripped out of my chest and thrown away. I gave up my leg to play again and now it was over for me anyway. It took me back to the day I was told I had cancer, when I had thought I would never play again.

I stayed in the same spot for the rest of the game and couldn't stop crying. None of my teammates said anything to me. Again I felt like a ghost. Even after the game, I found it hard to get off the bench. My body was numb, and I couldn't move. I guess I was scared of what my future held without sports in my life. I was scared of that life. The days after that game were the toughest. I felt like I had no purpose, no goal. Without sports, my life felt empty.

Even with the disastrous season over, I still wanted that letter jacket. After school one day, I ran into Coach in the parking lot and decided I needed to once again say something because the jacket meant so much to me.

"Coach, I wanted to know about the letter jackets and if it would be possible for me to get one . . . ," I said.

The coach shook his head. "Oh—I'm sorry, Scott, I already placed the order for the jackets. I didn't know you wanted one." Trying hard not to lose it and break down in front of him, I turned and slowly walked away. The jacket I had worked so hard for was no longer a reality. It was devastating for me to accept that I would never get one.

15

FORGING A NEW LIFE

I could feel myself losing hope. I still had to go to Cook Children's for my checkups. A few days or even a week before each checkup, I would drive myself crazy thinking bad thoughts. I felt like I was doing too good for too long and that I was due for some bad news. I was scared to death that the cancer was going to come back, and if it did, there was no way I would survive it.

Every time I had a checkup, I would pray for good news. To me, I was either going to get told that I was going to live and be OK, or I was going to die. On top of going for the checkups, I was still getting used to life as an amputee. I had just as many checkups to fix this or adjust that on my leg, and my leg wasn't comfortable all of the time. I had days where my leg would ache, and it would be too uncomfortable to wear. I would have days where I didn't want to get out of bed and days where it felt like too much to put my leg on and get on with it. That was especially true if I was already sore and achy or if I knew my leg wasn't fitting right.

I had to accept that this was my life now. With baseball, I had a reason to get up and put my leg on. Now, with all that over, I had a hard time getting motivated and finding my purpose in life. I knew God had kept me alive for a reason, but at that time I didn't know what it was. This was one of the hardest times for me. The one thing I loved most—sports—seemed like it was out of my life forever.

Amputee or not, I'm still a guy, and one thing that will cheer a guy up no matter what is a girl being interested in him. To my surprise, a few weeks before I was to graduate, I was told by a mutual friend that there was a girl who thought I was interesting. She worked at the town's snow cone stand. I knew she didn't know I was an amputee because I always wore pants, but I decided to go with my friend and meet this girl.

When I saw her, I couldn't believe it. She was beautiful and seemed way out of my league. Of course, I had pants on, so I was not as self-conscious because my leg was hidden. My thinking at the time was that if I hid my leg she would never have to know that I was an amputee. If she didn't know, she would like me. I figured that if she saw my leg she would instantly become uninterested.

I met her and we hit it off. A couple of days later, we went out on our first date. That night I also got my first kiss, and I was blown away. I had always thought after the cancer and the amputation a girl would never be interested in me.

A month went by and she became my girlfriend. I was so happy when I was around her. All my worries just disappeared. I felt like I was living two different lives. I had the one when I wasn't with her and I was depressed, upset, scared, and fearful. And then I had the one when I was with her and I was happy and ignoring the fact that I was an amputee. It's true, I didn't like the fact that I felt like I had to hide my leg. I wanted to come out and tell her I was an amputee. I would understand if she didn't want to be with me, but I was so happy with her that I didn't want to lose her.

One day while watching television at her house, I got up the courage to just come out and tell her. As I explained the things that I had been through and confessed that I was an amputee, I became terrified of her reaction.

"I know," she told me.

"You know?" I asked in shock.

"Yeah, I've known the whole time. I knew before I ever met you. It doesn't bother me," she said.

"You've known this whole time?" I asked her. "I've been making myself crazy worrying that once you found out you would leave me!" I felt so relieved that she accepted me for me. I felt closer to her and found myself thinking that she was the girl for me.

I know it sounds crazy, but given what I had just gone through and thinking I'd never kind love as an amputee . . . this was a dream come true. I had come to think of myself as a freak physically. Having a girl-friend who was into me, really into *me,* made me feel normal in a way I had not felt since losing my leg. Being a teenager, you're always worried about how you look. With her, my whole attitude changed. I felt whole again. She made me feel so happy and so ac-cepted, I couldn't ask for anything more.

All of this was new to me. I was in love. But with young love comes heartbreak; after five months she wanted to end things. I didn't see it coming, and I quickly became depressed again. She broke my heart and broke it bad. With all the things I had been through, I could now add heartbreak to the list.

I found myself lost again, not knowing what to do. I had planned on attending a community college with her to take some classes to see what I might be interested in, but I dropped that idea after we broke up. With the depression came anger. At the age of eighteen, I felt like I had been through a lifetime of hurt. After graduation, the few friends I had made on the baseball team floated out of my life. I wasn't a typical teenager; I'd been through too much. I wasn't interested in going to parties every weekend.

The last place for me to find friendship was at my job at the grocery store, but that didn't last. As I said earlier, I was in want of friends—and probably a little too much. I was in search of any type of friend, so much so that I was acting like a different person. I ended up hanging out with people I would not normally have hung out with because I had no reason to steer clear of them. There was a group of people stealing from the registers at the store. I had nothing in common with these people, but I was desperate for friendship. I found myself falling victim to peer pressure, and I made a huge mistake.

When I first heard about the theft, I thought those guys were crazy. But the majority of the kids at the store thought it was the "cool" thing to do. I wanted to be a part of something that was cool. I did it a few times, and I felt horrible about it. I so badly wanted to belong to a group of friends that I looked for friends in the wrong places. I looked cool to the kids that worked there, but I didn't like how it made me feel. I knew it was wrong, and I hated it. I hated myself for doing it and for so desperately wanting friends. I was ashamed of myself, and I wanted out of that situation, so I quit working at the store.

I was also frustrated because I knew people really didn't understand what I had been through and why I was the way I was at times. I was always a shy kid, but with the things I had been through, my shyness and my lack of confidence had gotten worse. I wasn't the kind of person who could just go up to someone and make a friend. I just wanted to fit in and feel normal.

Being depressed, I lost touch with a lot of people. I was out of high school and had no immediate plans for college. I had a lot of time alone. One of the reasons I wasn't ready to go to college was because I didn't know what I wanted to do, and I just wanted a break. Going through the whole cancer thing and going back to high school and having to make constant adjustments made me emotionally exhausted. During this time off, I would still shoot hoops at my house. When I got to feeling down and out about things, I would shoot some hoops. It made my troubles disappear for a while, and it relaxed me. Everybody has their thing, and mine was going outside to shoot baskets. I was still not secure with myself.

I knew I had to go get a job and get out in the world. Plus, I was broke. One place I went to for a job was the outpatient therapy clinic where I had done my own therapy. They were located in a fitness center, so I figured I could get a front desk job. I went up there and met with the therapy tech, Jeff, who had worked on me and helped me with my therapy. We chatted and got caught up, and I asked him if he knew if the fitness center was hiring for the front desk. He didn't think so, but he thought I would be great in the physical therapy department.

"Don't you have to have a degree for that stuff?" I asked him. "Not to be a therapy tech," he said. "It's pretty much on-the-job training. Let me see what I can do for you." A month later I had an interview, and a week after that I had the job.

As a therapy tech, I would assist the physical therapist as needed with taking a patient through their exercises, helping out with office work, cleaning the gym, and being available to other staff members. My first day on the job I was really nervous, but I quickly learned different types of exercises so that I could help patients get through their programs.

Everyone I worked with at the clinic was extremely nice and helpful. When they asked about my story, I would tell them all about what I'd been through, and they were amazed by my accomplishments and my drive. It helped me to see the amazing person inside of me.

For some reason I had never seen overcoming cancer as a big accomplishment. The fact that I got right back to sports didn't register with me either. People told me I was strong, and I was flattered by their remarks, but I saw it as something I had to do. I hadn't had have a choice. The only thing for me to do was to just do it. I could've given up, but I didn't, and that fact helped me to see myself as strong and impressive to others.

A month into my employment, I got a call asking if I would be interested in running the relay torch for the winter Olympics. A few days later, I received an Olympic jogging suit that I was to wear for the torch run. Getting that in the mail convinced me that it was actually going to happen.

I was later told that Dr. Murray had nominated me to run the torch. He thought I would be a great candidate since I was a cancer survivor who loved sports.

I would be the main person that was going to end the run into Austin. Until the day of the event, I wasn't told who I would be handing off the torch to at the end of my run—I was only told that it was some-one famous. As I watched the television coverage of the other torch runs across Texas, I saw that most of the celebrities were professional athletes. When we arrived in Austin it had been raining most of the day. I was to run .2 miles, which is about halfway around a high school track. My torch run wasn't until mid-afternoon, so we got there early and mapped out the place I was going to run. I was also set up to do a few local media interviews for a number of television stations.

This was pretty exciting. I felt like a star. That whole morning, I went from interview to interview, sharing my story over and over again. The rain had begun to die off, but the roads were still wet. My time was coming up for my run, and I got on the bus to take me to my spot. While on the bus, I was handed the torch. It was amazing to see it in person, and I was truly overwhelmed by the enormity of the fact that I was running the Olympic torch. I had been through something terrible, but I was still here. It was start-ing to hit me that I had overcome a huge hurdle in my life. I was a survivor. I had lost half my leg, but I didn't let that stop me from my goal of getting back to sports. I felt honored to be given the opportunity to run the Olympic torch.

As the bus came to a halt, the marketing guy that was riding with me asked me if I knew who I'd be handing the torch to. I told him no. "Well, just so you can prepare yourself for when you get there, you're going to be handing off the torch to Lance Armstrong," he said with a grin. My eyes went round with shock. How exciting! I was going to hand the torch over to Lance Armstrong! The reason they wanted me to run last was so I could hand it to him, one cancer survivor to another.

As I exited the bus, there were people everywhere. I saw my parents and my family, along with Dr. Murray, all standing on the sidewalk with cameras in hand. All up and down the sidewalk, on both sides, there were people pressing in. As I walked off the bus, I was greeted by two people in purple jogging suits with ear pieces. I later found out that these guys were with the Secret Service and would be running along with me.

The atmosphere was indescribable and breathtaking. In my right hand I held my torch, waiting for the other person to arrive and light it. It was a dream come true, especially for someone like me. With the roads still wet on the downhill route, everybody was convinced I was going to walk. I must admit, it did cross my mind. I watched as a woman in the same jogging suit came running towards me with her torch. My time was coming.

I was told as she was running towards me that she was Lance Armstrong's wife at the time. As she came closer, I made up my mind to run the route when my torch was lit. I had been through so much to get me to this moment and I was going to go all out.

When my torch was finally lit, I began my run down the slick hill. I could hear my mom and aunt in the background saying, "Oh my God, he's going to run. Hurry up, so we can get it on film!" They chanted, "Go, Scottie, go!" The whole time I was running, I just kept telling myself, *Don't fall!*

When I finally made it down the hill and around the corner towards the Capitol, the crowd got bigger and bigger. There were cheers and applause roaring from the crowd and about twenty police motorcycles lined up. I was blown away by what I was seeing. I was directed by the two guys running with me to go in front of the capitol building, where an Olympic torch stand stood ready for me to place my torch in it as we waited for Lance to arrive.

There must have been a hundred or so people crowded around and just staring at me. It felt like everybody was waiting on me to say something, and of course, nothing came out of my mouth. I was shocked by the size of the crowd. I looked around with a smile while trying to catch my breath.

"Good job, that was awesome. How was the run?" someone from the crowd yelled out.

"It was good. The torch is heavier than it looks," I joked. A few more minutes passed, and I could see Lance riding in on his bike towards the crowd. A few kids were riding along behind him. As he arrived, he was met with a huge round of applause. He got off his bike and walked towards me with his torch in hand. We shook hands and greeted one another. Again, I was at a loss for words. I was meeting a guy who had overcome cancer and was back doing what he loved. Not only had he gone back, he dominated his sport.

It was a huge honor for me to meet Lance Armstrong and to light his torch. Just as quickly as we meet, the flame was passed from my torch to his, and he was off on his bike to ride the torch through the streets of Austin. The second he took off on his bike, a ton of television cameras and microphones popped in front of my face. It was like a press conference. I took question after question about my run and how I came to carry the torch. I felt amazing. I felt like an athlete again. Like the torch, my inner athlete had been reignited. I got to keep the torch. To me, it was like a trophy. Just as the NBA and MLB have trophies for world champions, the torch was my trophy for beating cancer. I'd had the toughest, hardest, and longest game of my life, and the torch was my winning trophy.

When I returned home the following day and got back to work, I showed off my new trophy. With the praise, love, and support I got—not only from my family, but my coworkers too—I was beginning to feel better about myself. I still wore pants, and I still had issues with the way I looked, but my coworkers were starting to see a change in my behavior. Accordingly, one of the other techs—his name was Brian—started trying to get me to wear shorts to work. Summers in Texas are hot, but no matter the temperature I still wore pants. I was always sweating all the time and was very uncomfortable. Everybody at work was wearing shorts except me.

One day I decided to give it a try and finally found the courage to wear shorts, showing off my leg. Brian told me not to worry because everybody already knew about my leg. It wasn't going to be a big deal. The next day, I walked into work wearing shorts. This was a huge step for me. My coworkers were very kind. They made me feel comfortable and treated me the same. When I went to go help a patient with their exercises, the questions started to come. I had worked with this particular patient many times in the past, always clad in pants.

"Scott, if you don't mind me asking, what happened to your leg?" asked the patient.

"I had cancer when I was younger and had my leg amputated so I could get back to sports," I explained.

"I've been coming here for a month and I would never have guessed you had a prosthetic leg," the patient said. "I think it's awesome to see someone who's survived something like that and is OK walking around with their leg showing. You're an inspiration to me. Thank you." For the rest of that day, I had patients telling me the same thing. For them to see someone who had gone through hard times and was doing well helped motivate them to get better and stay positive. I never realized how much of an impact I could have on people. Having that kind of a positive impact on others helped me overcome some of my own insecurities. I continued to wear shorts from that day on.

I was now motivated to keep my dreams alive. I still had that dream of becoming a professional athlete. The depression had kept me down, but I was now beginning to see my potential. The torch run had a huge impact on me. Just as I was learning to live fully again, I got a phone call that would change my life.

16

CONSEQUENCES

The phone call was from a detective from the Joshua Police Department. He asked me if I could come down to the station to answer a few questions. As soon as he said it, I knew what it was about. I knew it was about the stuff that had gone down at the grocery store. I was a little scared because even though I didn't work there anymore, I wasn't sure what he was going to ask me.

The next day I made my way to the police station to meet with the detective. He was nice and friendly. When we got to his office, he asked me to have a seat.

"Scott, you no longer work at the grocery store, correct?" he asked.

"That's correct," I said.

"While working there, did you know of any illegal stuff going on?" he asked. I was now very scared. What with me being scared, I lied and told him no. "Well, Scott, the problem is that there has been a lot of money taken over a long period of time. Did you ever take money from the store?" he demanded.

I quickly said, "No, sir." He then placed on his desk a stack of papers saying that at least six people had confessed to taking money. All six had said I was a part of it. Hearing this, I was terrified for my future.

"Now, Scott, just be honest with me and you won't be in any trouble. You're young and people make mistakes. But if you lie to me, and we find out that you lied, you'll be in big trouble."

Hearing that, I knew I had to confess. "Sir, I'm sorry. I did take some money." I was so ashamed. "I didn't take a lot of money, but I did take some," I told him.

"About how much do you think you took?" he asked.

"I'm not sure, sir. It couldn't have been more than a hundred dollars," I said.

"Try higher than that," he said with a cocky smile.

"Sir, I'm being completely honest with you," I said. "I apologize for not telling you the truth at first but I was scared. I'm telling you that I did take some money but there is no way it was more than a hundred dollars."

He said, "Well, I appreciate your honesty, Scott. You're not going to jail. Like I said, young people make mistakes and we just want to get to the bottom of this. Would you mind filling out a confession? Basically, you write down what you just told me." In fear for my future, I agreed to fill out a confession. The whole time I was writing it, tears were rolling down my face. I was thinking about having to tell my parents and how disappointed they were going to be in me. I couldn't believe I had let myself get into this type of situation. I had made one of the biggest mistakes of my life and it was all because I was in need of some friends.

When I arrived back home later that day, I knew I had to break the news to my mom. "What's wrong, Scott?" she asked as soon as she saw my face.

"I need to talk to you about something. Mom, I'm so sorry," I said, crying. "I took money from the grocery store when I worked there and I had to go talk to a detective about it today. I didn't take any more than a hundred dollars, I swear. I had to tell him the truth because he said six people had stated that I took money."

My mother was frustrated. "Why, Scottie, why?' she asked.

"I was stupid. I just wanted so badly to fit in. The detective said I wasn't going to jail but I'm still scared," I told her. Even though my mom was disappointed in me, she comforted me. I could tell she truly understood why I had fallen into that kind of a situation. She knew the real me. When my dad arrived home, we broke the news to him. His reaction was about the same as my mother's—he was angry, but he understood.

It all felt so unreal. I was the happiest I had been in a long time, and now this was happening: would the nightmare ever end? As the month passed, I slowly got back to normal and began to believe that the whole terrible experience was behind me. I was at a good job that I enjoyed. I was opening up and having fun.

One day, I got a letter from the district court. When I opened it up, I read that I was being charged with theft of $1,500–$20,000. My heart sank. *This can't be happening.* I thought all this was over. My parents immediately set up a meeting with a lawyer.

The lawyer looked over the case and explained everything to us. It seemed that all six or seven of us that had been brought in that day for questioning and had given confessions were being charged with the same thing: theft of $1,500–$20,000, a felony. The reason each person was being charged with a felony was because they didn't know for sure who took what amount of money. They just had a total amount of money that was missing from the store and charged each person with that amount. There was no way I took anywhere near that kind of money. I had even confessed to the amount I'd taken—no more than one hundred dollars. The lawyer said if I was telling the truth, I was not guilty of the charge. But if they found me guilty in a court of law, I was looking at two years in prison.

How did my life go from beating cancer to facing prison? Once again, I felt like I was fighting for my life. While all of this was going on, I was still working at my job. I was a mess, but I couldn't let it show at work. I didn't want anybody to know. I had made one mistake and it was coming back to haunt me.

About three months later, my lawyer came to me and said that the DA had come to him with a deal. I could go to trial and take my chances or I could take deferred adjudication. With the deferred adjudication, I was to perform 120 hours of community service and pay $2,000 in fines along with monthly probation fees. He then told me that once I completed the terms of my deal, the crime would be taken off my record. I quickly chose to take the deferred adjudication.

I was not a criminal, and I knew I wasn't going to put myself in that kind of a situation ever again. As the months passed, I still had my job at the hospital, but I now had to pay fines every month, complete my hours of community service, and check in once every two months with a probation officer. This part of my life was embarrassing and very hard on me. I didn't want people to know about this because, like I said, the crime was not me. I felt like I had to hide everything about my life: hide my leg, hide my bouts with depression, and hide my legal woes. I felt if people knew the whole truth, they would only see the negatives. They would see my leg missing, my legal situation, and my insecurities, and they would see me in a different light. I wanted too much to be accepted by people and it got to me. Yet even though I was going through all of this, I knew I had to keep my dream alive.

17

NOT THE PARALYMPICS

When I had my Hanger appointments with Phyllis, I would express to her my continuing drive to be an athlete. She mentioned that I should try track and field with the Paralympics, the big sporting event for amputees and other special needs athletes. This being my only option, I agreed to try it out.

Phyllis and I made the trip to Oklahoma City to meet with the other Hanger people to see about getting me into the event. When I first met the Hanger people, they were excited to meet me. They had heard from Phyllis that I was an extremely active guy. They sat me down, asked me some questions, and then asked if I wanted to run in the Paralympics. I told them I was interested.

Without them seeing me run, they immediately placed a contract in front of me to be sponsored by them for over four years. I was shocked. These guys didn't even know if I was good enough to compete and they wanted to sponsor me. I was expected to train and run in a few track meets to prepare for when the Paralympics came around. I was given a fancy running leg that had a J-shaped foot without a heel. I also found out about how much that running leg cost: at the time it was around $50,000.

The first time I ran on that running foot, it made me run faster. It pretty much springs you forward. When I agreed to train and run at the track meets, Hanger agreed to sponsor me. I would get help with my leg and I would promote Hanger. It was kind of like being the athlete I wanted to be. While going through the training process and getting into the sport, I quickly realized that track and field was not for me.

I never was into the whole track and field scene, and the only reason I was doing it then was because it was one of the few professional sporting events for amputees. Just the few times I went to the local high school track in my city, I didn't like anything about it. It just wasn't me. I felt like I was doing something that I knew I was going to dread. It wasn't fair to me and it wasn't fair to the people who were going to sponsor me. I had to get out of that sport.

I asked one of the guys at Hanger in Oklahoma if there was any type of stand-up amputee basketball. He told me there was no such thing. He cited issues like getting enough amputees together to play in the same area and the high level of activity required by the sport. I didn't have much to say but I'm sure my emotions gave me away. I was upset and baffled by the fact that there was no league. Knowing that my heart was not into it, I felt it was best to let the guys at Hanger know that I wanted to drop out before the first big track meet.

It was hard to drop out, and Phyllis could see that I was really struggling, and she said she would ask if there was any such league around. To my disappointment, I was told that a league like that had never come about. Even with this news, I continued to play ball constantly at my house. The Paralympics wasn't for me.

DREAMS COMING TRUE

I knew in my heart I wanted to be an athlete. One of the main reasons I had decided to cut my leg off was so that I could continue to play and compete in sports. Other people pushed me towards college but my heart belonged to sports. I knew what I wanted to do: I wanted to start my own basketball league. It made perfect sense to me. I'd had the odds stacked against me before and now I was facing the odds of losing my dream. I knew I had to start my own league. I couldn't ignore the drive and the passion in my heart.

Phyllis asked the people at Hanger if they could help me with my dream. I was told once again that it would be too hard to start. I was angry. If there were amputees out there running track, there were amputees out there playing basketball. As time went on, I kept thinking of new ways to get the word out about the league. I made flyers along with a letter detailing my dreams and goals for the league and mailed them across the United States. I sent them to the media, to prosthetic companies, to sports organizations, and to celebrities like Mark Cuban, Oprah Winfrey, and well-known athletes. I sent out hundreds of letters and got one reply: from a marketing person with the NBA. He thought my league was a great idea but was unsure of how to help me get started, so he directed me to the wheelchair basketball league.

I got in contact with them and didn't get much help. Instead, they tried to recruit me to play for them. I refused to play because that defeated the purpose of my league. I wanted to play basketball standing up. I had beat cancer, been through rehab learning how to walk and run again, and they wanted me to sit in a chair and play basketball? It was very frustrating. I have nothing against the wheelchair basketball league but I am not in a wheelchair. I play all the time with my prosthesis, so it only made sense that I wanted to start a stand-up league.

I was finally in college but I was still not sure of what degree I wanted to get. Like I said, my heart belonged to the dream of becoming an athlete. To play what I wanted to play—stand-up basketball—I had to compete against able-bodied athletes. It made me a better player. Needless to say, I believe that amputees should have their own professional sports. It could be just as big as able-bodied professional sports. It would give hope to someone who had lost a limb to know that they could still become a professional athlete. A stand-up amputee basketball league would show people that amputees can do anything, opening the doors for other kinds of amputee professional sports.

What good is a high-tech knee, foot, or prosthetic leg if I'm playing basketball in a wheelchair? I can do anything or play anything that I want. With this league, I want to give hope to children and adults who had lost a limb. I wanted them to know that there are other options than just track and field.

Just because I lost my leg doesn't mean I have to lose my dream. I dream of this league constantly. I know I was kept alive for a reason. I feel that reason is to inspire others. I want to give hope and motivate others to keep going and to never give up. The league would represent that to others. You would have people in the league that had overcome trials in their lives willing to play for the love of the game and not for the money. There was no doubt in my mind that a league such as this could be the next big thing in sports.

Watching amputees playing basketball, standing up, would definitely give the public something to look at. People are constantly amazed by my high-tech leg. As I dream about this league, I can see everything happening in my head. I know that one day I will find the right people who will believe in my dream and give it a chance. I can see the public coming in droves to witness amputees playing stand-up basketball. I dream about this league becoming a professional league. I dream about it becoming mainstream with televised games. I want it to be mainstream because you hardly ever see amputees on television. I think if there were more amputee sports out there to watch, fewer people would be freaked out when they saw someone with a prosthetic leg. It would help people in my shoes feel better about being an amputee.

To show something real, inspirational, and motivational would provide a fresh new face for professional sports. I know a basketball league like this will take time and effort. It's not going to happen overnight. But I know in my heart that this league would be successful if given a chance. I will not give up on this dream. I didn't give up when I was diagnosed with cancer. I didn't give up when I had my leg amputated. I have come too far to stop now.

Thinking about all of this, I took the next step and made a video of myself playing basketball, showing people exactly how it's done. I felt if they actually saw me playing, they would get it.

My friend Brian is a big film guy. He loves to shoot and make videos and has a real passion for it; we met one year at camp. Brian had the same cancer as me, same leg, same doctors. He agreed to shoot and post some footage of me playing basketball on the internet to show people that an amputee can play basketball standing up. We placed the video on YouTube along with some interview footage. As soon as we posted the video, the responses started rolling in from all over the country. I knew I was onto something.

The perfect plan came to me: A group of amputees traveling the country, playing stand-up basketball and raising money for charity. I figured at least one dollar of any future ticket sales or merchandise sales would automatically go to our own charity, a charity that would provide financial relief to cancer patients and amputees of all kinds. I knew firsthand how ridiculous the bills could be and how hard it was to get financial aid.

Then I thought of the name I wanted to call it: Amp 1. I chose Amp 1 because our tour would be kind of similar to the And 1 tour, but with "Amp" short for amputee. When people heard Amp 1, my hope was that they would automatically think of And 1 and think of basketball. The first message I got from an amputee was from a guy named Tyler in Utah. The message read, *Call me ASAP! We need to talk. Please call me!*

When I called Tyler for the first time, it was like I was talking to myself. We had both been wanting something like this for so many years and had the same frustrations about wheelchair basketball. We quickly teamed up and formed our own company, Amp 1 Stand Up Amputee Basketball. We know this will be successful.

Soon we started our own website, along with a MySpace page. The great big domino effect we'd been waiting for began to happen. I had amputees from across the country telling me how much I was inspiring them and how they couldn't wait for our tour to become a reality so they could watch us play. Before we knew it, we had a total of ten guys from across the country interested in playing with us—all this from a YouTube video and a website. We were even getting asked to play at Rucker Park in Harlem, New York, once we had a team together. This was huge! I had never dreamed we'd get a chance to play at a legendary basketball court. Just think of the people we could reach and the interest we could generate—not to mention gaining a few much-needed big-name sponsors.

Imagine a basketball league where every player has their own story to tell about how they overcame the trials in their lives to become who they are today. Nothing has been handed to them and they refuse to accept excuses not to play. They have an incredible love for the game of basketball and a passion to help others through difficult times.

Amp 1 makes the statement that anything is possible. All you need is courage, motivation, determination, and the heart to follow your dreams. The difference between able-bodied athletes and amputee athletes is heart, not limbs—and we don't take anything for granted. While touring, a major goal of Amp 1 Basketball would be to visit hospitals, clinics, and rehabilitation facilities to provide inspiration, motivation, and hope to people. A second goal of Amp 1 Basketball would be to arrange speaking engagements to share some of our stories and show how with faith, hard work, and dedication, anything is possible. Amp 1 athletes are dedicated, motivated, committed, hardworking, and inspiring people. We can make a huge impact in the sports world and touch the lives of millions across the country.

I feel very fortunate to be where I am today. I can't thank my parents and family enough for the love and support they continue to give me. There just aren't enough words to express the love that they have shown me and the care that they have given me. I am truly blessed to have them in my life.

Phyllis and the people at Hanger are talented and gifted people. They helped me keep my dream alive and provided me with the tools of the prosthesis to get back to doing what I loved. Phyllis never once said I couldn't do anything and always believed in me and my dreams. If it wasn't for people like her, I wouldn't be back to doing the things I love, all the while chasing my dream.

Cook Children's Medical Center and Camp Sanguinity also gave their love and treatment to help me fight cancer and to be the survivor that I am today. I owe everything to them. From Dr. Murray to everyone that helped care for me, they were angels watching over me and slowly curing me of cancer. I continue to thank God for everything that they did for me. I am so thankful that I had Dr. Murray as my doctor. I put my life in his hands and did everything he told me. In my eyes, he is the best doctor in the country. He treated me like a friend and believed in me the whole way. If I ever doubted myself, he was quick to tell me that I could do it. He's one of the big reasons I'm still here today.

I wanted to write this book to share my story and to provide hope and faith to all of those who experience tough times in their life. There is always someone worse off than you, and God doesn't give you more than He knows you can handle. I feel fortunate to have gone through what I've been through because it has made me into the person that I am today.

The five years that I faced on my deferred adjudication are now complete. It's still embarrassing to talk about, but I felt I needed to put the event in my book. It was a big event that happened in my life and one I still have to deal with at times. When I sat down to write this book, I made it a top priority to leave that part out. But while writing it, I felt that I needed to put it in here. I know there are kids out there in similar situations: fighting cancer, losing friends, and feeling alone in the world. I wanted to show them what happens when you make the wrong decision. I don't want another kid to fall as easily into that kind of a situation as I did. Having cancer at a young age, you're still just a kid. You're growing as a person, all the while facing a life-threatening and life-changing disease. It's a hard battle. I hope that my sharing my experience will show kids everywhere what can happen when you try too hard to make friends in the wrong places.

I have learned many things about myself, especially how strong I can be—I was strong during my cancer fight and I continue to be strong today. I will never give up on my dreams and goals. I may get knocked down, tested, and battered and bruised, but I will continue to be strong.

I get asked all the time what keeps me going and what drives me. There really isn't an exact answer. Everybody has their own thing that motivates them to do the things that they want to do in life. I know what I went through was tough, but it was not the worst thing in the world. There were many things that could have gone wrong. I could have had cancer in my lungs; I could have had my leg amputated at the hip; I could have lost my battle with cancer. It's the children who inspire me to keep doing the things that I'm doing. I see myself in them, and I want to be a role model to them, always giving them hope.

Tomorrow is never promised. I went from football practice one day to having cancer the next day. I went from having two legs to having one. You never know what life is going to throw at you, so you have to have faith in the man upstairs and know that no matter what happens in your life, it is for a reason. You may not understand the reasons, but it is all for a higher purpose. I had to learn to leave things in God's hands. Nobody can control everything. I didn't choose to have cancer, but I feel I was given the disease for a reason, and I believe that God doesn't give you more than you can handle.

With everything I've been through, I sometimes feel that I have the right to be angry. But with my dream still in my heart and my passion for helping others, I know I don't want to be angry anymore. No matter how long it takes me and no matter how many hurdles and obstacles I face, I can't give up.

I will end by describing a recurring dream of mine . . . .

I'm in the locker room getting ready for the first Amp 1 game. I look around and see all types of amputees. There's a guy just like me, a guy with a below-the-knee amputation, and a guy with one arm. I put my leg on, I make sure it's on good and tight, and then I put on my basketball shorts. I lace up my shoes. I can hear the music booming in the arena. It's close to game time, and the announcer is hyping up the crowd. I look into my locker, and there's my jersey. It reads "Amp 1" across the front. I turn the jersey over to put it on, and the back reads "Odom 3 ½." I pause for a moment. I'm overwhelmed with emotion. The dream is coming true. I put the jersey on and we all start to make our way down the tunnel. As we get to the end we stop and get ready for our introduction. The arena is pitch black. Boom-boom clap. Boom-boom clap. *Music is playing over the speakers. The crowd starts to roar louder and louder. I get chills. It's the happiest moment of my life. A video is playing on the big screen, displaying our names. A shot of me comes up, quickly fades out, then finally shows me with a basketball in my hand and a look on my face that tells the world everything I've been through to get to this point. We make our way out of the tunnel, and the crowd gets louder. I look around the arena and see the fans cheering us on as if it was the NBA finals. I see young amputee kids with huge smiles on their faces. As we make our way onto the court, I look around and smile. With that smile comes a few tears. I was tested by cancer. I was tested to see if I still had it in me to be the athlete I wanted to be with my prosthesis. It hits me—I lost my leg, but I never lost my dream.*

ABOUT THE AUTHOR

Scott Odom is a very busy guy. He works full-time at Huguley Memorial Hospital as a wound care technician. Along with his full-time job, he spends countless hours working to turn Amp 1 into a household name. Along with Tyler Hyatt, Scott has made it a mission to make Amp 1 Basketball his full-time gig some day.

Scott edits and posts all the videos that are on Amp 1's YouTube page. Along with Amp 1, Scott loves to give motivational speeches. Whether it's to schools, organizations, or a small group, he never turns down the opportunity to spread his message: never give up.

Along with work, Amp 1, and motivational speaking, Scott is also pursing a college degree. He's in his final year of getting his bachelor's degree in psychology from the University of Phoenix.

Scott's dream for Amp 1 is for it to be a household name and for amputee athletes to be seen in the same light as able-bodied athletes. The main goal Scott has for Amp 1 is to build a league like the NBA—a league where amputees are seen as athletes, not disabled or challenged athletes. It has taken nearly ten years for Scott to get to this point, to see his book published. No matter how long it takes, Scott will continue to pursue his lifelong dream, no matter the odds.

SPONSORS PAGE

"A New Era in Publishing" ™

Fort Worth, Texas: My first team sport, flag football. If you are wondering which kid is me, I'm the one holding the football. Age 5.

October 1997. One day after coming home from my amputation surgery. I wheeled myself to the court at my parents' house to shoot some baskets.

Christmas 1997 at Cook Children's Hospital. I had the opportunity to meet one of my favorite football players, Troy Aikman.

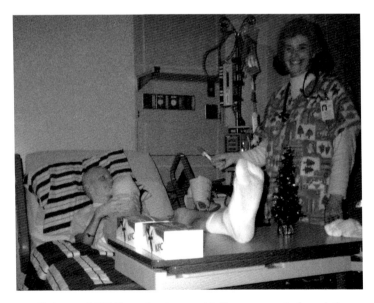

Christmas 1997. I'm trying to sweet talk my way out of my daily medications with one of my favorite nurses. I didn't win. Age 14.

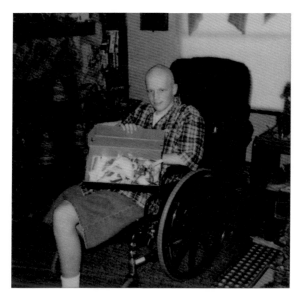

Three months after being diagnosed with cancer. I'm holding a box
full of hospital wristbands I've collected since my diagnosis.

Christmas 1997. I was doing my best to keep my mind off
of things and not let my emotions show. At the time, I feared it
would be my last Christmas with my family.

Early 1998, at my parents' house. I was so physically
weak that it became difficult to get from my bedroom
to the bathroom just across the hall.

Summer 1998. Throwing out the first pitch at the
Texas Rangers game against the Seattle Mariners.

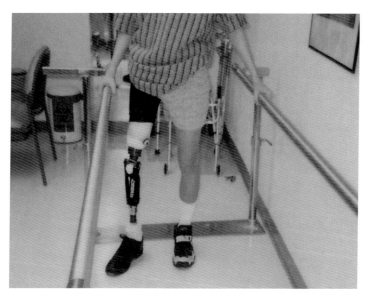

Late 1998. Getting fitted for my first prosthesis at Hanger Prosthetics, starting the long road of learning to walk again.

May 2001. Pitching in the last game of my senior year of high school. This was the most difficult and emotional game I have ever played.

May 2001. A soon as I looked my mom and dad in the eyes,
we all knew that this was going to be my last baseball game.
It was a very emotional moment for us.

Summer 2001. Climbing the rock wall at Camp Sanguinity.

December 2001, Austin, Texas. Handing off the Olympic Torch to fellow cancer survivor Lance Armstrong. Dr. Murray, to my left, nominated me for this once-in-a-lifetime opportunity.

Summer 2004, Camp Sanguinity. Me with one of the camp's teen leaders, Dawn Arnold, showing off my new "Cancer Survivor" tattoo.

Dream coming true. This is just the beginning. From left to right:
Brian P. Vincent, Jovan Booker, Myles Davis, Scott Odom,
Ray Gurriere, RJ Dozier, and Tyler Hyatt

Team Amp 1. The half numbers on the jerseys are
meant to show fans the team's sense of humor and their
comfort level with missing half of a limb.